HUNTING MISSOURI'S

Whitetail DEER

RON GOODMAN

Paperback-Press
an imprint of A & S Publishing
A & S Holmes, Inc.

ISBN-13: 978-1-945669-70-5

CONTENTS

INTRODUCTION

"Hunting Missouri's Whitetail Deer" is designed primarily for the beginner deer hunter, but hopefully the seasoned hunter will find something new and interesting to consider, or will at least be reminded of something forgotten along the way. The author felt there was a need to address the fundamentals of deer hunting in an easy-to-read handbook form. It's directed primarily to those interested in hunting whitetail deer in Missouri. However, the basic behavior and habits of this magnificent animal are fairly consistent wherever they are found in similar habitat.

I am grateful to the many people who helped me with this project. I am especially thankful to the Missouri Department of Conservation, and the individuals associated with it, for answering so many of my questions, and allowing me to use information and illustrations from some of their publications.

I would also like to thank my wife and family for their patience and help. But most of all, I am thankful to Almighty God, who created all things and allows us to enjoy His handiwork!

Increasing our knowledge and skill can be an exciting and rewarding experience. Hopefully, this handbook will help some of the many deer hunters like myself who enter the woods each fall in pursuit of this elusive animal.

Some years ago, a young man who had never been deer hunting and knew practically nothing about it, was asked if he would like to go. He accepted his friend's loan of an 8mm rifle and half a box of shells. After firing a few practice rounds and purchasing a deer tag, he entered the woods on opening day. The morning was cold and rainy. Though he knew very little about deer or deer hunting, he knew enough to seek protection from the weather in a nearby cedar thicket. Fortunately for this greenhorn, at about the same time a young buck was entering the same thicket from a different direction, obviously for the same reason.

A few minutes later, the lucky "deer hunter" had the crosshairs on his first deer. This young man, who just a few days earlier didn't know a whitetail from a muley or a rub from a scrape, much less how to field dress a deer, was now a bona-fide deer hunter, standing next to his truck proudly displaying his un-field-dressed, four-point trophy. Unfortunately, there are many deer hunters in the woods each year who get their start in a similar fashion; not necessarily as lucky as the one in the story, but often knowing very little about whitetail deer, or how to hunt them.

The Hunter Safety Program, which is required for all aspiring deer hunters born on or after January 1, 1967, is good preparation and can provide the foundation for a lifetime of rewarding experiences for hunters. There has probably been more research and writing done on the subject of whitetail deer than any other big game species in North America, and yet we are all still learning. This is the way it should be.

Good hunting, think safety.

Ron Goodman

(Ron is the one on the right)

HUNTING MISSOURI WHITETAIL DEER

According to the excellent publication, *Whitetail Deer Ecology and Management*, compiled by Lowell K. Hall, there are five species and many sub-species of deer in North America. In Missouri, we have the Kansas Whitetail, a large deer with heavy antlers. They are cautious and very alert creatures. Whitetail deer are considered by many to be one of the most difficult big game animals to hunt. The degree of success enjoyed by deer hunters in Missouri is due primarily to the large number of deer available (the Missouri Department of Conservation [MDC] estimates the deer population to be over a million as of 2016), the large number of hunters in the woods during firearms season, and the knowledge and skills passed on from hunter to hunter.

Along with the whitetail's curious nature, they're able to detect the slightest movement; but their sense of smell is their chief defense, rivaling that of a bloodhound. They are powerful animals with tremendous endurance, yet graceful and agile. Even a heavily-antlered buck can lay his head back and run through wooded areas we'd have difficulty walking through. They can jump an eight-foot fence, and are good swimmers. Whitetail deer get their name from the white underside of the tail. When alarmed, a running deer raises its tail, waving it from side to side ("flagging"), which reveals the large area of white hair, warning other deer of danger.

The reddish-brown hair of their early summer coat fades to light brown as summer progresses, and is replaced by a longer, thicker, grayish winter coat. The process is reversed in spring. The white spots on a newborn fawn are only on the tips of the summer coat, and will fade away as summer progresses. There are only a few true albino deer in Missouri. Albinos are pure white with pink eyes. Deer can also be piebald, in which case the normal coat includes patches of white. Rarest of all are melanistic deer, which can be very dark brown to completely black, depending on how much melanin is in their skin. The average height of an adult Missouri whitetail doe is 36 inches at the shoulder, bucks a few inches more.

Normally, adult bucks in Missouri weigh approximately 150 pounds, and does a little less. The deer that holds the record as the heaviest ever taken in Missouri weighed 369 pounds. This monster buck was killed in Livingston County in 1954 by Clifford Davis. An even larger buck was taken in 1970 by Dwain Perrige of Edina, Missouri. Field-dressed, this deer weighed 361 pounds, and its estimated live weight was 423 pounds. Although the scales were checked and witnesses verified the weight, officials were not present at the time of the weighing; therefore this buck was not listed in the record book.

Missouri ranks high among states producing big bucks. Many have made the record books, and Missouri currently holds the #3 position for bucks with typical antlers, and the #1 position for non-typicals. That particular buck, known as "The Missouri Monarch," was found in St. Louis County in November, 1981. The deer had apparently died of natural causes. Its massive non-typical rack scored 333 7/8 points shown below. Because this buck was found dead and was not killed by a hunter, there was some debate as to whether or not it should appear in the record books. Eventually, this deer was officially recognized as the #1 non-typical whitetail, at that time, in North America.

No. 1   Non-typical: North America

In addition to national conservation organizations such as the Boone & Crockett Club for firearms and the Pope & Young Club for archery, our state has its own clubs that keep records of trophies taken in Missouri. The Show-Me Big Bucks Club and Archery Big Bucks of Missouri both honor hunters who take outstanding trophies in the state. To have a trophy checked by one of their representatives, contact the wildlife division of the MDC.

GENERAL BEHAVIOR

I've watched and studied whitetail deer for many years. I've talked to experts like Tim Russell and others with the MDC, read and used (with permission) the Department's printed material on the subject of deer behavior. I've discussed the habits of whitetails with other knowledgeable people such as Don Baker, owner of the hunting lodge "Ozark Mountain Ranch" in Dixon Missouri, Don Harris from Bass Pro Shops in Springfield, Missouri, and others devoted to the study of this remarkable animal. One thing's for certain, phrases like "all things being normal," "most often," and "as a rule" must frequently be applied to statements about deer behavior. In other words, even though whitetail deer are creatures of habit, they are also extremely adaptable, and often alter their routine for various reasons.

Deer, especially bucks, become more active just prior to and during the rut, which usually starts around mid-to-late October. No one seems to know exactly when it starts or ends, but the peak of the rut is usually mid-November. Their normal routine of feeding at night and bedding down during the day is altered somewhat during this time, and it's this general restlessness and sometimes careless behavior (especially by dominant bucks) that give hunters such an advantage during the rut. However, as hunting season progresses, deer adapt by coming out later and later in the afternoon.

It's difficult to predict how a mature buck will respond to an approaching hunter. Does and young deer will almost always run, but an adult buck might bolt, sneak away, or just sit tight and watch you pass by. If you stop for any length of time, a buck might try to slip around behind you to check you out.

Normally, deer do not travel far in their daily routine. If sufficient food, water and shelter remain available, they will probably live their entire lives within a one or two mile area, except for an occasional visit to a distant field of grain or alfalfa, or doing a bit of extra roaming during the rut. If normal conditions prevail, and barring drought severe enough to affect the water supply, major wildfires, the encroachment of humans or other such pressure, this home range probably won't change much from one generation of whitetails to the next.

DISPERSAL

Whitetail family groups are composed of does and their offspring from past seasons. Although most young deer remain within their family groups, as the numbers increase some of the young ones will strike out and form groups of their own. When a doe is ready to give birth she likes to be alone, and often drives away her offspring until the new fawns are born. Yearlings returning to their mother are sometimes ignored or treated as intruders, causing some to leave permanently. A mixed group of young deer from various families gather and form a new herd. The young bucks in this group are especially affected, now having spiked, forked, or even small six or eight point racks.

Feeling their oats, but being rejected by family and harassed by older bucks, they are ready to strike out on their own. The young ones that do stick around are usually accepted back into the family.

Bachelor Groups

During the spring and summer months, you may observe several large bucks hanging out together. Although there is definitely a "pecking order" within this bachelor group, they usually get along quite well together while growing their new set of velvet-covered antlers. Bucks are somewhat reclusive and relatively mild-tempered during this time, and tend to be careful not to injure their growing antlers, which are easily damaged at this stage. When the antlers have finished growing, the blood stops circulating under the velvet and it becomes very dry. Bucks begin rubbing it off against small trees and shrubs ("antler polishing"). This is much different than the aggressive rubs that bucks make later on, just prior to and during the rut. During that time, any former group-mates who encounter one another often become fierce rivals.

FEEDING HABITS

Like most animals, whitetails are creatures of habit. Except for during the rut, their daily routine is fairly predictable. Even though trails from bedding areas to feeding grounds can be found throughout the whitetails' range, clearly safety is their primary concern when moving from place to place. This is evident by their use of cover that could offer protection as they travel to and from their feeding grounds. They normally travel in a group to the feeding area, and once there they separate and browse in a scattered, loose herd.

Deer require water daily, and usually have several sources within their home range. Whitetails are very fond of new growth, such as new shoots, buds, new leaves and ivy (including poison ivy). They eat the flowers and stems from fruit trees, and are especially fond of such things as apples and persimmons. Although they enjoy grass, especially bluegrass, they do not digest it very well. Unfortunately, they don't seem to care for fescue, which stays green later in the year than other grasses.

They also enjoy mushrooms, lichen and other mosses, the red berries on buck brush, other berries, wild grapes and wild roses. These are just a few of the many things that whitetails eat. Farmland crops are definitely on the menu. As winter approaches and food becomes scarce, deer will consume almost any vegetation they can find, including dead leaves, twigs, vines, hedge apples, and even the bark of certain trees. Acorns make up a large part of the whitetails' diet, and barring a late spring frost or severe drought, they are abundant from mid-summer through early winter.

According to the MDC publication, *Missouri Oaks and Hickories,* there are fifty-four sub-species of oak trees. Twenty-one of them can be found in Missouri. The acorns on eight of them are classified as sweet, having the least tannic acid. These are the White Oak, Swamp White, Bur, Post Oak, Chinkapin, Swamp Chestnut, Dwarf Chestnut, and Overcup. Deer will eat all acorns, but prefer the sweet.

White Oak

Swamp White Oak

Bur Oak

Post Oak

Chinkapin Oak

Swamp Chestnut Oak

Dwarf Chestnut Oak

Overcup Oak

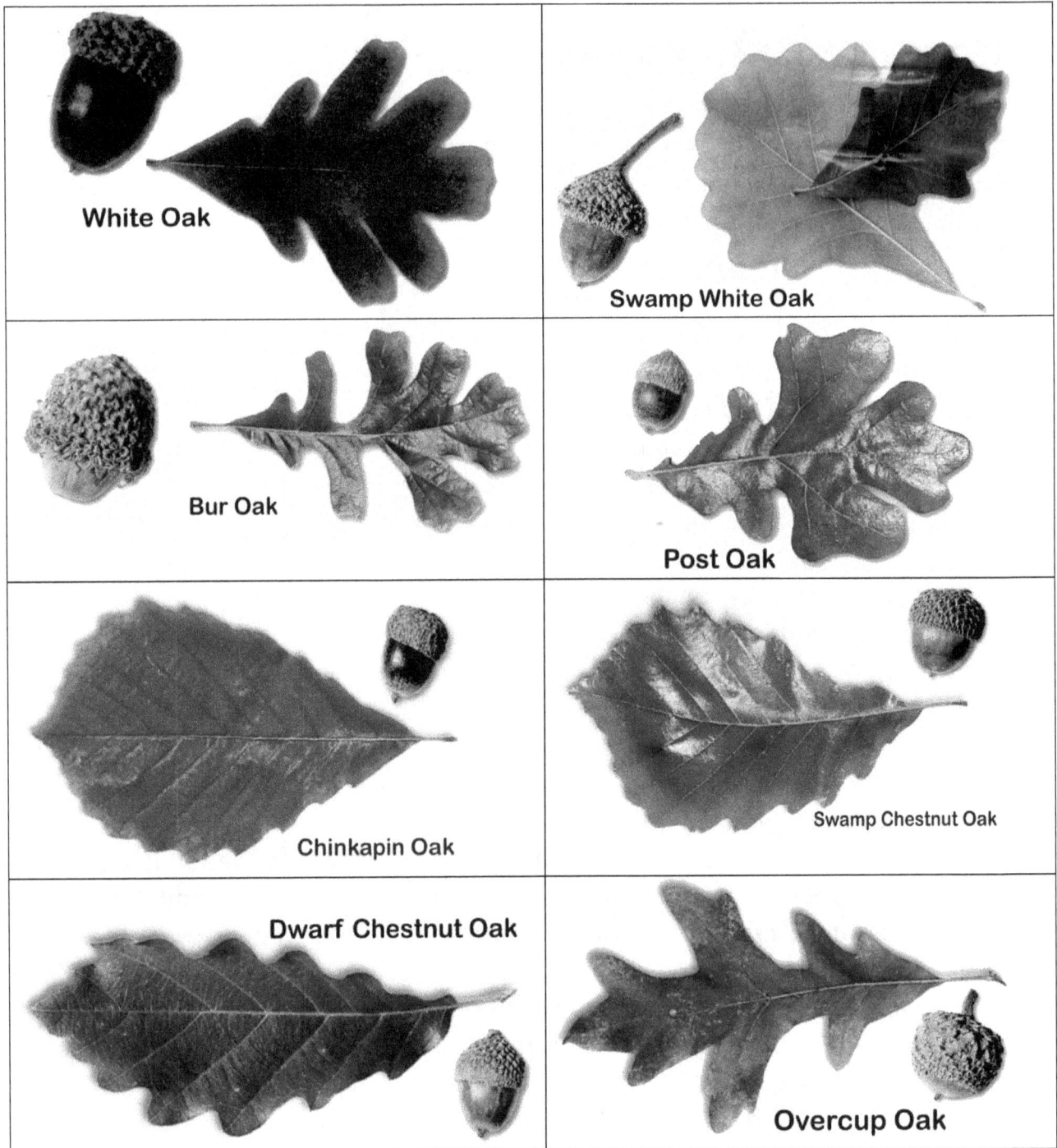

Round tipped leaves mean sweet acorns.

**Pointed Tipped
Oak Leaf**

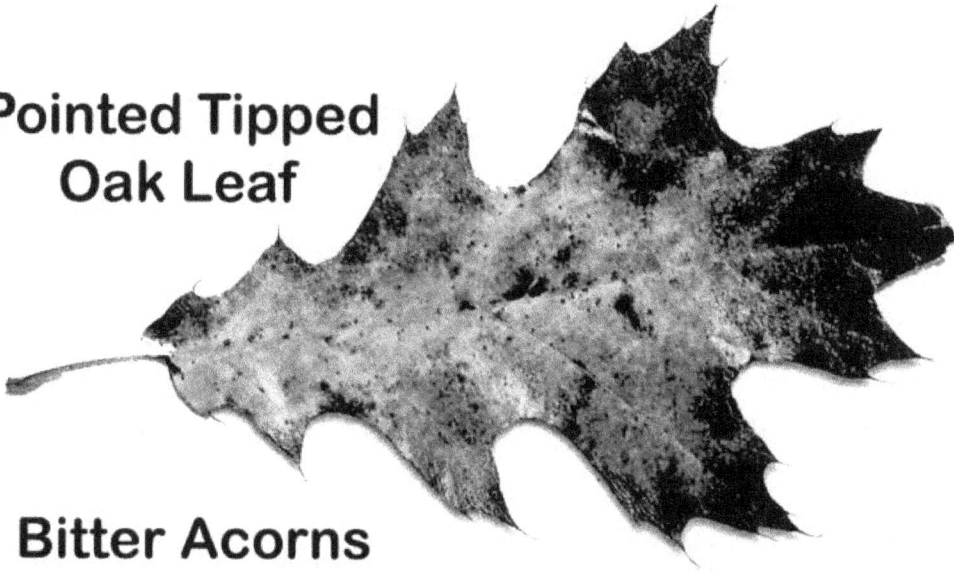

Bitter Acorns

**Rounded Tipped
Oak Leaf**

Sweeter Acorns

Oak trees that produce sweet acorns can be identified by their leaves, which have rounded tips. The tips of leaves on trees producing bitter acorns are more pointed. The exceptions to this rule are the Blackjack and Water Oaks, which have round-tipped leaves, but the acorns are bitter. Leaves on the Shingle and Willow Oak are unlobed (having no tips), and are also bitter.

Shown here are pictures of leaves, to help you find the trees that produce the acorns that deer prefer.

Blackjack Oak	Water Oak
Shingle Oak	Willow Oak

These four oak trees have round tipped leaves but produce bitter acorns.

How do you identify a dogwood tree?

By its Bark!

Under normal conditions, deer start moving into their feeding areas late in the afternoon and will feed off and on throughout the night. Around daylight, they begin returning to their bedding area. While resting during the day, deer spend some of this time chewing their cud, grooming themselves and each other, and may occasionally get up, move around and do a little browsing close to the bedding area. Although the night is spent feeding, deer also rest off and on during this time.

They don't return to their daytime sleeping area, they simply lie down wherever they happen to be when the impulse strikes. This routine may be altered by such things as stormy weather, rutting activities, or the presence of hunters. When scouting an area for hunting, try to do it as close to opening day as possible, to find the hot trails leading to the current feeding area. Be careful not to disturb or leave your scent near any trails, scrapes, or rubs so the deer don't alter their routine.

To determine what the deer in your area are feeding on, check the contents of the stomach during field dressing. A deer has four parts to its stomach: The rumen, the reticulum, the omasum, and the abomasum. The rumen, the largest chamber, is where you can find identifiable food.

COMMUNICATION

Deer are not aggressive as a rule, but as with most wildlife, dominance prevails among whitetails. This is easy to see among the bucks, but not as obvious among does. In determining dominance, the size and age of the deer play important roles. Even though deer normally get along quite well together, fights can break out for various reasons.

Aggressive behavior among whitetails mainly consists of pushing with the head and kicking out with one front foot. A more severe action is rearing up and flailing with both front feet. Once dominance has been established, it normally takes nothing more than a look from the dominant deer to make its subordinate tuck tail and step aside.

Whitetail deer communicate through body language as well as vocalizations. A relaxed whitetail carries its tail down, flicking it occasionally, for reasons unknown. When the deer is alarmed, the tail goes up, displaying a large area of white hair around its rump. The underside of its tail is white. As the animal runs away, its tail waves back and forth, showing the white hair as a clear warning to other deer. This is called flagging. If a whitetail is more suspicious than alarmed, it may raise its tail slowly before leaving the area without flagging. When a buck is on the trail of a doe in heat, or a doe is searching for a fawn, or a young deer is playing, the tail may be held straight up, or partially up. If you see a doe holding her tail tightly to one side as she walks, she's probably being followed by a desirable buck. A tucked tail is a sign of a submissive, sick, or injured deer.

When deer are suspicious but not sure of the danger, they sometimes paw or stamp the ground. They may stare at an object (such as a hunter) and bob their head up and down. If they cannot make the object move in response, they may move a short distance and make a blowing sound. If the object remains unidentified to them, they may resume feeding, but are more likely to leave the area.

During the rut, a buck following a doe in heat occasionally thrashes his head into low hanging branches and saplings. He will sometimes lower his head and make a low, hog-like grunt as he walks. Other vocalizations include squealing or groaning when injured or in distress. A doe searching for her fawn calls with a low "mew." The fawn responds with sheep-like bleats. Deer also snort and grunt, for various reasons.

For example, when a deer is startled, it may snort and run simultaneously. When encountering an intruder, a deer may stamp its foot or paw the ground, sometimes making a combination snort/blow, trying to invoke a response. It is thought that the snort/blow has the effect of wetting the deer's nose, increasing its ability to identify the object by scent.

Since grunting is a sound often made by deer, hunters may want to purchase one of the many grunt-calls on the market. They come with instructions about which sounds to make, and how to make them. While grunting is most often used during the rut, it can work any time of year. A loud blow from a deer call can sometimes stop a running deer momentarily.

BUCKS, DOES & FAWNS

Whitetail bucks are typically heavier than does of the same age, being broader through the chest, and a little taller. When bucks reach maturity at five or six years of age, they will have developed a more boxy or rectangular shape than does. In the first autumn of a buck's life, most have developed a set of button antlers, so small they may not even break through the skin, but can be felt just under it. The following year, a buck should have spiked or forked antlers, or even a small six or eight point rack (the six or eight pointers are likely to become trophies someday). Bucks begin shedding their antlers around the first of the year, depending on their physical condition. Bigger, healthier bucks tend to keep their antlers a little longer than smaller, less healthy bucks. Antler sheds are consumed by rodents and other critters for the calcium and phosphorus.

"I much prefer cheese, but every time I take a bite, I get a sharp pain in the back of my neck."

New antlers begin to develop in spring or early summer, as food becomes available. Antlers grow throughout the summer, faster than almost any other living tissue, up to ½ inch a day. Antler growth depends on both the quality and the quantity of food available in the spring and early summer. As this food supply becomes available, nature meets the buck's nutritional needs first, restoring weight lost over the winter.

After that, much of his normal nutrition intake goes towards antler development. Since bucks recovering from rutting activity require more food to regain weight and strength, a long hard winter and a late, cool spring can be detrimental to antler development that year. Nutrition is an important factor in determining the size of a buck's antlers, and ancestry influences the shape—how tall, wide, the number of points, and whether a rack is typical or non-typical. When bucks compete for does during the rut, large antlers help, but more often it's body size, weight, and endurance that determines the outcome of a fight.

A yearling buck that has access to sufficiently high nutrition and yet develops only spike antlers may be deficient in some way, incapable of ever growing desirable antlers. In places where deer hunting is big business and trophy-sized racks are in high demand, bucks that develop only spikes in their second year are often eliminated from the privately owned herd.

Unlike the western mule deer, points on both sides of the rack are counted on whitetail bucks. Occasionally a whitetail doe will develop a set of antlers. According to the MDC, several of these antlered does are found in our state every year.

Some six or seven month old bucks are capable of reproducing, depending on their physical development at that point. At that age, the only breeding they're likely to achieve is with a lingering doe, while older bucks are fighting or distracted in some other way. Whitetails reach their prime at about five years of age, and retain this vigor for the next several years. It's practically impossible to determine a buck's age by his antlers after he has passed the button stage, unless a deer has reached very old age and his antlers are beginning to deteriorate. About the only reliable way to determine a whitetail's age is to check the lower jaw teeth wear. The color of the antlers, the amount of gray on the face, and other so-called age indicators are unreliable. Although whitetails may live longer in captivity, they seldom live more than ten years in the wild.

As the rut approaches, bachelor groups begin to break up, and big bucks often become competitors. Although whitetails can be very challenging to hunt, the rutting season brings about a new dimension in the behavior of this normally cautious and elusive animal. When a doe is ready to mate, she will visit one or more scrapes made by bucks in the area. By then she probably will have attracted the buck that made the scrape, and others as well. Trouble is brewing. When the dust settles and the victor has passed his DNA on to another generation, the buck and the doe separate. Unlike mule deer, whitetail bucks do not gather a harem of does. Pregnancy lasts six or seven months. In April or May, the doe will give birth to one, two, or occasionally three white-spotted fawns weighing four to seven pounds each.

This spotted coat, plus the fact that a newborn fawn has no scent except to its mother, enables fawns to spend their first few weeks well-hidden among leaves and brush. After about two weeks, fawns begin sampling grass, buds and twigs. By two months, the fawn's digestive system is sufficiently developed to subsist entirely on vegetation and other regular food, although they may continue to nurse. Occasionally a hunter is surprised when field-dressing a doe to find milk in her udder. The presence of this milk does not mean her fawn is depending on her for survival, she's just permitting it to continue nursing after it has been weaned.

By mid-summer, the white spots on a fawn's coat begin to fade, and will soon disappear altogether. Fawns stay close to their mother until the mating season begins in the fall. As a doe comes into estrus (heat) she often chases her fawns away, and reunites with them later. On average, forty percent of does in Missouri come into estrus during their first fall. The larger and healthier the fawn, the more likely she is to come into heat her first year. Deer in the northern part of Missouri tend to be larger than those in the south. A fawn that has grown to about eighty pounds is most likely to experience an early estrus.

Whether in her first or second year, once a doe begins bearing young, she should continue to do so for the rest of her life, as long as she remains healthy. The first pregnancy usually produces a single fawn, and in following years twins are common. Rarely, but occasionally, a doe will have triplets.

There has been considerable debate as to the degree of color blindness in whitetails, but most agree that they are unable to distinguish color, seeing only shades of light and dark grey. It's very unlikely that they can see the "hunter orange" we're required to wear. Glossy material is easier for them to see than dull orange.

GLANDS

Shown here are four of the visible glands that play a major role in the lives and communication of whitetail deer.

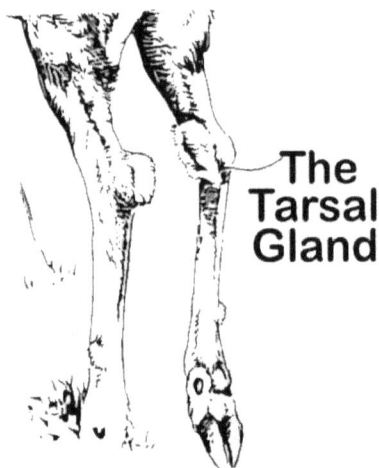

The Tarsal Gland

TARSAL GLANDS: These are located on the inner surface of the back legs. They secrete a musky odor. During the rut, a buck will stand over his scrape and let urine run over these glands onto the scrape to get the attention of a doe in heat. Young deer will sometimes urinate on these glands out of fear, and adult deer may do this as an expression of anger, or a sign of aggression. During the rut, this gland and the hair around it will be stained very dark. Be careful not to get any of this on the meat while field dressing your deer.

METATARSAL GLAND: The purpose and function of this gland is not as well-known as other glands. Since it is located low on the outside surface of both back legs, it probably marks the spot on the ground where the deer was lying. When the deer is alarmed, the hair around this gland flares outward and releases an odor, leaving a scent trail as the deer moves through grass or brush. When flared out, the white hair can clearly be seen by other deer.

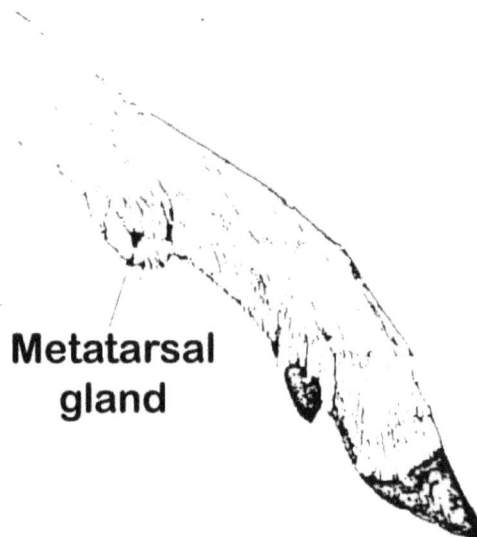

Metatarsal gland

Interdigital gland

INTERDIGITAL GLANDS:
These are located between the split hooves of a whitetail's foot, and secrete a waxy substance every time a deer steps down, identifying its tracks to other deer.

PRE-ORBITAL GLAND:
This seems to be little more than a tear duct. Bucks have been observed carefully depositing substances from these glands on shrubs and brush, especially on low hanging branches above a scrape.

Preorbital gland

Forehead glands also play an important role, but are not visible on the deer. These are used to leave scent on rubs, brush, or whatever the deer wants to "mark." The nasal glands are located just inside the deer's nose. They are believed to contribute to whitetails' powerful sense of smell by keeping the nose moist. The pituitary gland, located behind the eyes at the base of the brain, measures the amount of daylight in a twenty-four hour period. It has a big influence on rutting activity.

THE RUT

Some of the older, larger fawns are capable of breeding in their first fall, but as a rule, they don't start until their second year. Breeding only takes place during the rut. It's difficult to predict when the rut begins, but it's usually mid-to-late October. The peak of the breeding season in Missouri is mid- to late November, even though some breeding may continue through December because of fawns coming into heat later than the older does, and the does that didn't get pregnant the first time around.

The pituitary gland, located in the head just behind the eye, measures the amount of daylight that passes through the eyes. Once this light decreases to a certain point, testosterone levels increase, and rutting activity begins. Obviously, bucks are ready before the does, having antlers polished, territories established, and rubs and scrapes prepared before does begin to show any interest in participating.

During the rut, a buck's neck swells to almost twice its normal size. He seems to have one thing on his mind, and is willing to sacrifice sleep, food and common sense to accomplish it. Does are in full heat for twenty-four hours. Most are bred right away, but if a doe is not pregnant after her first heat, she will come in again twenty-eight days later. She will only tolerate the attentions of a buck when she is in full heat. If a buck senses a doe is nearly ready to mate, he will stay with her, fighting off rivals until she is ready.

When a buck's time with the doe ends, he may track down one of his rivals and challenge him for his doe. If he cannot chase his rival off with a look, a fight will probably ensue. This is primarily a pushing contest, with body weight and strength making the difference. Antler tines may break off during the scuffle, but serious injuries seldom occur, although if a buck should slip and fall, the outcome could be serious. Usually, one buck will simply tire and walk away. When the fight is over, the winner seems to have little interest in pursuing the loser. A dominant buck may spend so much energy defending his doe, fighting off rivals, and breeding, that it's not uncommon for him to lose up to twenty percent of his body weight during the rut.

Rubs

Within a buck's territory, he'll make numerous rubs by scraping his antlers against small trees until the bark is shredded. His forehead glands leave his scent on the rub. These rubs are more vigorous than rubs made earlier, to remove velvet. These bark-shredding rubs can easily be seen from a distance, and serve as a guide to does, as well as putting other bucks in the area on notice. Other unusual rutting-buck behavior includes sparring with small trees and brush, possibly depositing his scent on them also.

Scrapes

A buck will create a scrape on a relatively flat surface, close to trails between bedding areas and current feeding areas. He will paw away the debris to the bare ground, making a spot one or two feet in diameter (sometimes much larger), then stand over it in a half-squatting position and urinate, letting the urine pass over the tarsal glands on each back leg onto the scrape. As a doe enters her estrus cycle, she may visit one or more scrapes, leaving her scent on each one. Bucks frequently check their scrapes for signs of a visiting doe. Unfortunately for him, rival bucks may leave their scent on his scrape as well. When a buck finds his scrape cluttered with the smell of other bucks, he may try to paw the dirt out and urinate on the fresh ground, or he may simply make a new scrape a few feet away. If there are low-hanging branches over a scrape, a buck may thrash his head into these branches, depositing scent probably from both his pre-orbital and forehead glands. Bucks often begin making these rubs and scrapes days, or possibly weeks, before the does are in full estrus.

Watching a scrape can be worthwhile, especially during the period just prior to does coming into estrus. That's when bucks are becoming impatient, checking their scrapes frequently. Not only may you spot the buck that made the scrape, but does and other bucks that are checking it out as well. If the buck that made the scrape is with a doe, he may not return for a couple of days or more. When watching a scrape, be careful not to leave your own scent too close to it.

While an enlarged neck and stained tarsal glands are sure signs that a buck is active in the rut, another indicator is his strange and sometimes careless behavior. A buck may be so focused on pursuit of a doe, he may not notice a hunter that's close by. If you're specifically hunting a buck, and a doe comes meandering along, be careful not to spook her. There's a good chance the buck you're looking for isn't far behind. Given the chance, some of the young bucks will participate in rutting activity, but after being constantly discouraged by older, more dominant bucks, they're not as totally preoccupied with it as the older bucks.

Larger than average scrape.

REGULATIONS

According to the MDC, regulations are for the protection of the species, safety, and to ensure equal opportunities for sharing. Laws regarding deer hunting change frequently, and it is the hunter's responsibility to be familiar with current rules and regulations. These are made available prior to each season in the pamphlet, "Fall Deer & Turkey Hunting Regulations," found wherever tags are sold. Here are some of the well-established laws that have been around for a while, but even these are subject to change.

Those owning or leasing and living on at least five acres of land, who plan to hunt on that property, qualify for various no-cost permits. However, they must abide by the same rules as other hunters, including tagging and checking in their deer.

Outer garments (hat, coat or vest) that are solid "Hunter Orange" must be worn during firearms season. Camouflage orange is not legal. (Note: your hunter orange garments should be dull. Although deer do not distinguish color, they may be spooked by glossy material).

A deer must be checked in by 10pm on the same day it was killed.

Hunting deer from a public road and hunting from any motorized vehicle (including a boat with a motor attached) is illegal in Missouri, as are the use of live decoys, electric calls, and dogs. However, dogs can be used to retrieve a mortally wounded deer. Special rules apply.

It is illegal to shoot a deer while it's in a body of water, nor can you put a deer carcass into a body of water to cool it, or for any other reason

.

Fine Money Supports Missouri Schools

Fine money from *Wildlife Code* violations go to a designated school fund in the county where the violations occurred.

All hunters born on or after January 1, 1967, must complete and pass the Hunter Safety course to be eligible to hunt alone. Those who have not taken or passed the course may hunt with a qualified hunter. Check the regulations.

Neither a fully automatic rifle nor one with a capacity of more than eleven cartridges is legal in Missouri. Alternate method rifles (such as black powder) must be 40 caliber or larger.

It is now legal (as of 2017) to use a crossbow during archery season.

Hunting seasons for many species of small game coincide with deer hunting season in Missouri. There are special guidelines that apply to hunting small game during this time.

For a complete list of regulations, visit mdc.mo.gov/about-regulations. Remember, "a spike or a doe taken by the book is better than a trophy by hook or by crook."

FIREARMS

A good deer rifle doesn't need to be excessively high-powered. Where the bullet hits the deer is more important than how hard it hits, or how fast the bullet is traveling. A .222 or .223 would be a little too small, and a magnum is probably not necessary, since most of the shots in Missouri are less than 100 yards, especially in the southern part of the state. For many years, the .30-.30 has been the most popular rifle for deer hunting in Missouri, and may still be. The hinge, bolt and lever actions are popular, because of their dependability. The pump can be reloaded without taking it down from the shoulder for a quick second shot. Some prefer the semi-automatic for the immediate availability of the second or third shot. According to the MDC, many whitetails are taken each year with shotguns and slugs.

A bullet's energy is its striking force, its velocity is the speed of the bullet, and its trajectory is the curve of its path. Some of the things to consider when selecting a deer rifle are sufficient energy at long range, a flat trajectory, ease of handling, weight, and the cost and availability of ammunition.

A 30.06 rifle firing a 180 grain soft nose bullet is used in this diagram. These figures do not apply to any other rifle caliber, type or grain of bullet.

A 30-06 rifle firing a 180 grain soft nose bullet is used in this diagram.

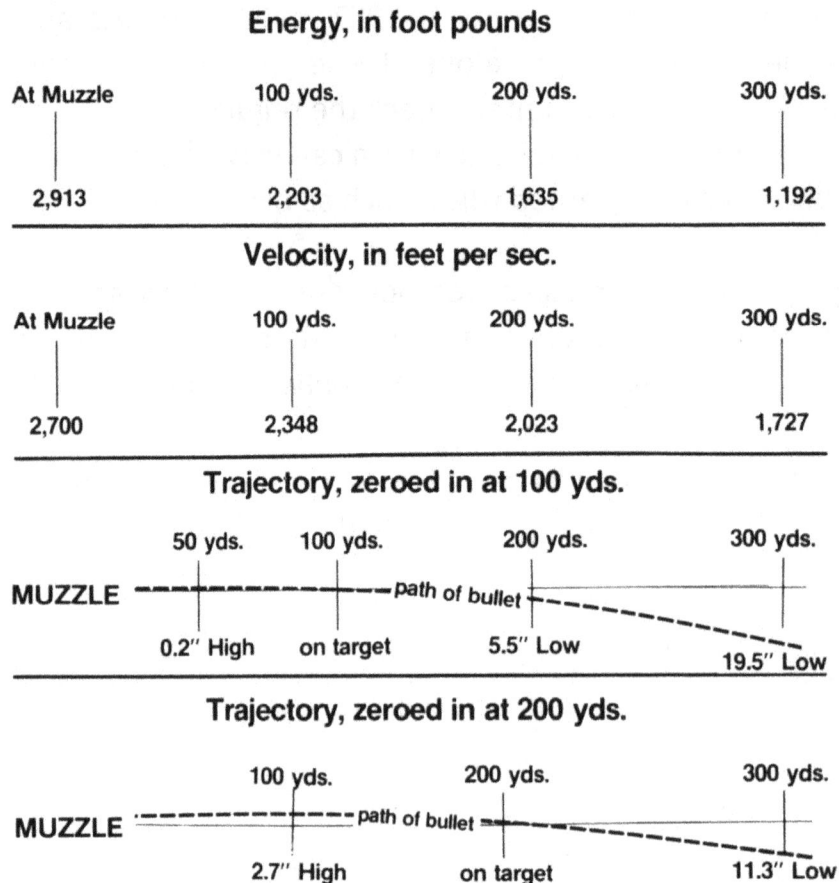

Energy, in foot pounds

At Muzzle	100 yds.	200 yds.	300 yds.
2,913	2,203	1,635	1,192

Velocity, in feet per sec.

At Muzzle	100 yds.	200 yds.	300 yds.
2,700	2,348	2,023	1,727

Trajectory, zeroed in at 100 yds.

MUZZLE — — — — path of bullet — — — —

50 yds.	100 yds.	200 yds.	300 yds.
0.2" High	on target	5.5" Low	19.5" Low

Trajectory, zeroed in at 200 yds.

MUZZLE — — — — path of bullet — — — —

100 yds.	200 yds.	300 yds.
2.7" High	on target	11.3" Low

Semi-Automatic action

Revolver action

It's important to keep all firearms clean, especially muzzle loading (black powder) guns. Some like to clean them with warm soapy water, and others prefer regular bore cleaner. Whatever you use, be careful not to leave any moisture that could come into contact with the powder. Every part of the gun must be dried thoroughly, including the threads on the breech plug. I know from personal experience that it doesn't take much moisture to cause it to misfire.

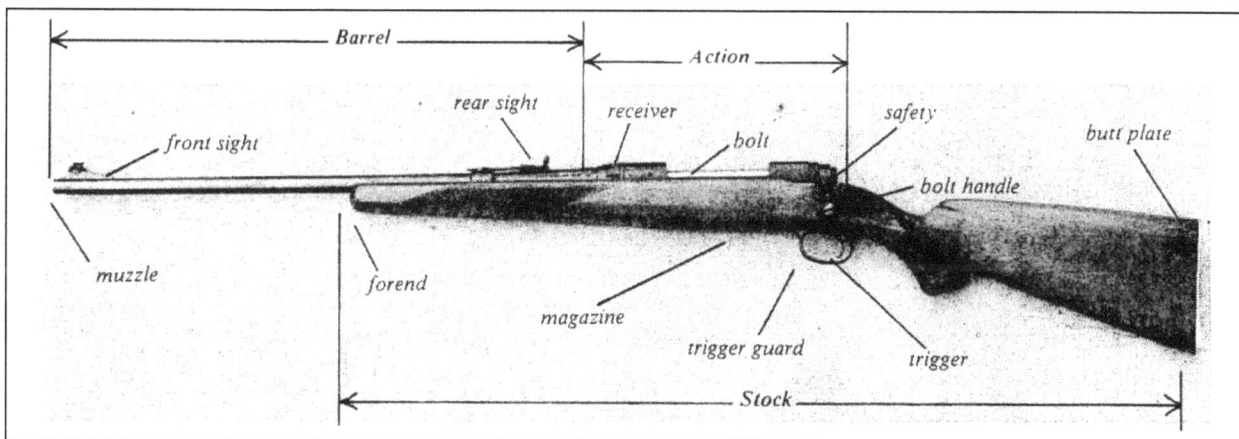

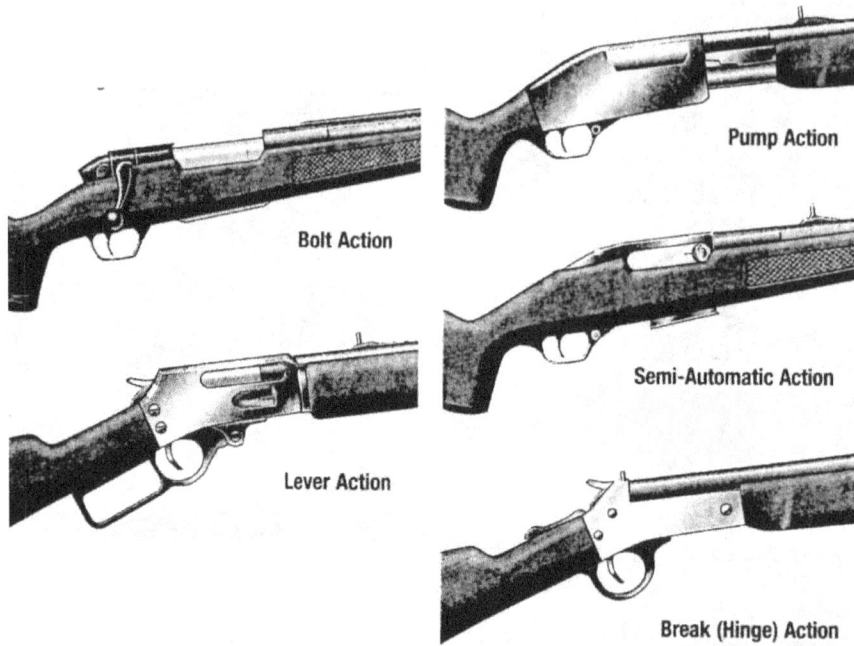

Bolt Action

Pump Action

Lever Action

Semi-Automatic Action

Break (Hinge) Action

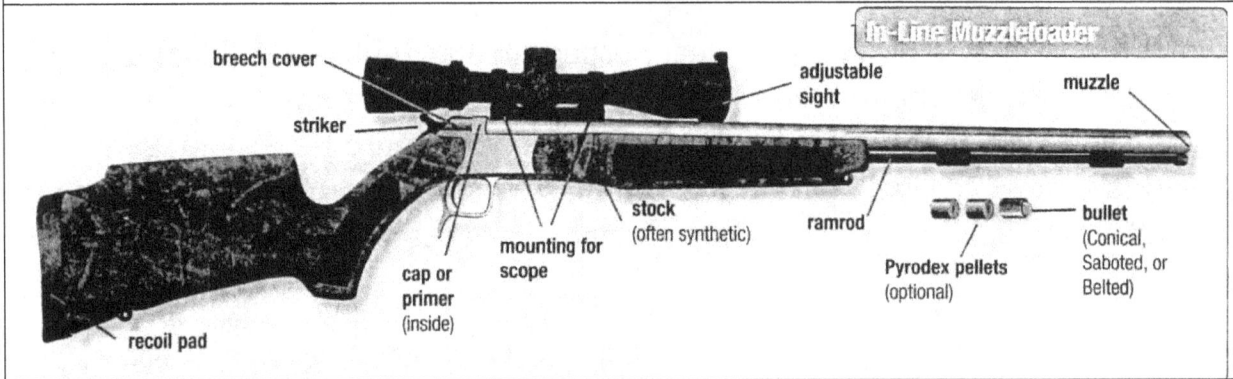

In-Line Muzzleloader

breech cover

striker

adjustable
sight

muzzle

mounting for
scope

stock
(often synthetic)

ramrod

bullet
(Conical,
Saboted, or
Belted)

Pyrodex pellets
(optional)

cap or
primer
(inside)

recoil pad

Scopes (Telescopic Sights)

One advantage of a scope is the simplicity of the crosshairs, as opposed to lining up the front and rear open sights perfectly every time. There are scope mounts that provide the option of using either the scope or the open sights. A "break over" mount is hinged, and can quickly be moved aside, exposing the open sights, then snapped back into place. A "side mount" is made for rifles such as the .30-.30. Winchester Model 94, which ejects the empty shells straight up. Probably most popular is the "see-through" mount. It is positioned above the open sights, making either of them available.

One of the arguments against a scope is that it might fog up in damp weather. There are anti-fog wipes, pastes and creams, which work to varying degrees. Most quality scopes come filled with argon or nitrogen gas, which helps prevent fogging. A high-powered scope provides greater magnification, but reduces the area of vision. A low-powered scope gives less magnification, but a larger area of vision. Fortunately most scopes are variable. Some of the more popular variables are 1-4x, 2-7x, and 3-9x, but scopes that magnify up to 80 times are available.

On-Target

There's a big difference between sighting in a gun, and target practice. Before practice can begin, your sights must be right.

When firing your gun, instead of pulling the trigger, try to make a fist around it and squeeze the shot off. A steady squeeze makes the shot more accurate.

Fire a couple of rounds, then check your target. Using a pair of binoculars will save some time. If the bullet hits too far left, move the rear sight to the right. If the shots are too far right, move the rear sight left. Too high, move it down. Too low, move it up. When making adjustments, always move the rear sight in the direction you want the bullet to move to. Instructions for adjusting a scope are printed on the scope.

Once the sights are set, it's time to start practice shooting. The more you handle and shoot your firearm, the better shot you'll be. Instead of shooting offhand when hunting, try to find something to rest your gun on, such as a limb, a fence post, or against the side of a tree. Even resting the gun on a forked stick can make your shot more accurate.

When shooting downhill at a fairly steep angle, there's a tendency to shoot over the target. Judging distance can sometimes be difficult in wooded or brushy areas, where a deer often appears to be farther away than it would if it were standing in the open.

Trail Carry

While afield, especially if using the trail carry, be very careful not to get anything in the end of the barrel, such as snow, mud, or debris. A bullet traveling two or three thousand feet per second doesn't have time to push an obstruction out of the way, and is likely to split the barrel when fired.

CLOTHING

Wearing layers of clothes and staying dry are two things an outfitter would probably recommend if you want to stay comfortable in the woods, and be able to adapt to changes in the weather throughout the day. Wearing layers makes it easier to make adjustments by removing some things, and putting them back on later if needed. Of the many materials available, wool is hard to beat. It's warm, durable, and even when it gets wet, it can keep you warmer than most other materials.

THE HUNT

Deer have very good eyesight for detecting shapes and movement (especially movement). When you move, it should be in slow motion. It's hard to be inconspicuous in their territory, but leaning against a tree or being close to a solid object can help conceal your presence. Deer probably won't notice the orange outer garments you're wearing (be sure they're dull, not glossy), but your hands should be concealed in gloves, even in mild weather. I like to wear a camouflage net under my hat, which covers my face and the shape of my head. Never put "Doe in Heat" or any other deer lures (scents) directly on yourself or too close to your stand. You don't want deer looking right at you. Wash with unscented soap. Cedar needles rubbed onto your boots and clothes can help cover your scent (so does skunk oil, if you can stand it).

You can tell what direction the wind is blowing by tying a piece of cloth or thread to a limb. With the sun behind you and a slight breeze blowing toward you, you're all set.

Some time ago, a survey was taken that claimed most deer hunters fall into one of three categories: Forty-four percent are "utilitarian," hunting for meat. These hunters consider wild game as simply a crop to be harvested. Thirty-eight percent are "domanistic." These are the trophy hunters, who consider hunting to be mainly recreational, with an emphasis on competition. The remaining eighteen percent are "naturalist hunters," who love nature and the outdoors. They enjoy being out there on opening morning, anticipating a day in the woods followed by an evening around the campfire with family and friends, talking about the day's hunt. Most of the hunters I've talked to are a combination of these.

Each year, the MDC sets the dates and length of the deer hunting seasons. Presently, the regular firearm season lasts ten days, beginning on a Saturday and ending on the Tuesday before Thanksgiving.

NOT SO GOOD OLD DAYS

Deer hunting has not always been enjoyed in Missouri as it is today. In the early 1900's the deer herd was near extinction. In 1936, the MDC began a program to restore the herd by trapping deer in the most populated areas and relocating them to other parts of the state. From 1937 to 1957 they moved 2,343 deer to release sites in 54 Missouri counties (information courtesy of the Missouri Department of Conservation).

In 1944, the Department offered a two-day "bucks only" season. By 1951, thirty-two counties were open to hunters. In fifteen of them, the deer population was healthy enough to allow an "any deer" season. Slightly over 30,000 hunters took part, taking approximately 5,500 deer. By 1959, bucks could be killed in all counties in Missouri, and "any deer" could be taken in fifty-four of them. That year the harvest totaled 16,306 deer during the firearms season. Additionally, ninety whitetails were taken by archery.

By 1964, the annual harvest had reached the 20,000 mark, thanks to the good work done by the MDC. Part of that "good work" was the acquisition of 1.6 million additional acres of Missouri land, and the deer herd was restored to over a million. The annual harvest has increased steadily ever since. In 2015, firearms, archery and all special hunts resulted in 260,552 deer being taken. Despite the increasing number of deer killed each year, the herd continues to grow with a well-balanced ratio of bucks and does. The deer are generally healthy, and the future looks very good for deer hunting in Missouri.

WHERE THE DEER ARE

As a general rule, deer feeding off the farmlands north of the Missouri River grow larger than those in the heavily wooded areas in the southern part of the state. The southern counties produce more deer, but they tend to be smaller.

Whitetails spend a good portion of the daylight hours in and around their bedding area. Under normal conditions, mature bucks prefer a different type of terrain than does and young deer. Older bucks like to lie near the top of a ridge, taking advantage of the air currents that rise during the day and carry scents and sounds up to them. Does and young deer prefer the cover of thickets and brushy areas. During stormy weather or extreme cold, big bucks may move into these thickets temporarily. Just prior to bad weather, deer often become active for a short period of time, then lie down for the duration of the storm. It's not uncommon for deer to remain active later in the mornings following a stormy night. Deer that are disturbed repeatedly may seek heavier cover and become less active during daylight hours.

GOOD SIGNS OF DEER

When looking for signs of deer in your area, look for beds made in tall grass, or leaves and grass flattened in a large circular shape. Look for hair on barbed wire, deep prints where deer have jumped the fence, and those all-important rubs and scrapes. Look for fresh tracks and droppings. Deer droppings resemble those of rabbits, but are slightly elongated. When deer graze heavily on grass, rather than a more varied diet, their droppings become formless, soft lumps.

Finding tracks of varying sizes close together usually indicates that does and young deer are traveling in a group. A single set of large tracks could indicate a lone buck, but it's difficult to distinguish between a buck and a doe's track. A possible clue is that since bucks are broader through the chest than does, their tracks are a little farther apart. Also, large bucks do not pick up their feet as high as does when they walk. In an inch of snow or mud, a buck will leave lines behind his tracks, made by dragging the tips of his hooves as he walks. In deep snow or mud, all deer will leave these drag lines. Old tracks in soft ground can appear larger as the edges dry and pull away. In snow, the edges of tracks melt, which also makes them appear larger.

"Stand" Hunting

The three basic methods for hunting whitetails in Missouri are "stand," "drive." and "still." Of the three, *stand* is probably most often used. This kind of hunting requires a little scouting and a lot of patience. A tree stand overlooking a pre-scouted area, close to a trail, bedding area or feeding ground, can be very productive. Or some other good pace where you can stand or sit motionless and be able to adjust so the wind will blow toward you.

Once you've chosen your spot, try to be there before sunrise. Once there, move as little as possible. Be patient. Just because deer start heading back to their bedding place around sunrise, that doesn't mean you won't see them up and moving later. There are many conditions that can cause them not to bed down as they normally would, such as the general restlessness brought on by the rut, the presence of hunters in the woods, a shortage of food, or a morning following a stormy night.

Having confidence in your location is important. As time wears on with no sign of your prey, other places may begin to look better. As a rule, trusting in your pre-scouted location and being patient are more likely to pay off than moving around.

"Drive" Hunting

Driving, or pushing deer out of a thicket takes some planning, and the cooperation of everyone involved. For this, you need primary shooters (usually two), and any number of drivers. The shooters wait at the head of the thicket, one on each side, and should not change positions. The drivers enter the far end of the thicket, walking towards the shooters while making a racket to get the deer moving. They don't need to make a lot of noise, but enough so that the shooters know exactly where they are. Drivers also need to watch for deer hiding, or circling around behind them. After a shooter fills his or her tag, they should trade places with a driver. Filling a tag for someone else is illegal.

"Still" Hunting

The dictionary describes "still" as silent or without sound. That's a pretty good description of *still* hunting. The objective of this kind of hunting is to take a few slow steps, stop and look, take a few more steps, look, and continue until you see a deer before it sees, smells or hears you. Don't expect to suddenly see the whole deer. Look for any movement, solid shape, or the flick of an ear or a tail. Not only are you likely to see more deer using this method (even though it may be a flagging tail you're looking at), but you'll get more familiar with the territory. A pair of binoculars can be very helpful when still hunting. Using binoculars is also a good way to locate deer if you find fresh tracks in the snow or soft ground, and you want to do a little stalking.

A combination of stand and still hunting can be productive. Be on your stand early in the morning and again in late afternoon, but instead of returning to camp mid-morning, take a few snacks with you and do some still hunting through the mid-day. Not only do you get more hunting out of your day, it also breaks up the monotony of so much stand hunting, and you have the advantage of being on your stand while other hunters are heading back to camp, and returning to the woods later. That might stir up some deer and send one your way.

Tree Stands

There are definite advantages to hunting from a tree or some other elevation. Deer normally do not look up for danger. Your shape and movement are concealed better, your scent is more likely to be carried away from the immediate area, and you have a better view of your surroundings. However, it's not easy to sit or stand on a limb for hours, and there's always the danger of falling out of the tree. A portable tree stand, designed for comfort and safety, is a good investment. Tree stands are particularly effective when bow hunting. Permanent stands are not allowed on Conservation land. Unattended stands must be labeled

with a name and address, or a Conservation number, and can only be up from September 1 to January 31. Check current regulations for any changes.

Courtesy of Missouri Dept of Conservation: *Never carry your gun or bow with you as you climb. Use a rope to haul up your bow or unloaded gun after you're safely in your stand and hooked into your safety harness.*

You may encounter wild hogs while you're hunting. The MDC once recommended that all wild hogs be shot on sight. Now it requests that hunters do not shoot them, since it only scatters the herd. If you see wild hogs, report their location, so they can be dealt with effectively.

Feral Hogs

Feral hogs are highly destructive and prolific pests. They cause significant damage to wildlife habitat, compete for food with native species such as deer, prey upon native wildlife such as quail, destroy nests of native birds such as turkeys, degrade natural areas and agricultural lands, pollute ponds and streams, and spread diseases to livestock and people. Feral hogs are a menace that must be eradicated in Missouri.

Report Feral Hogs. Don't Shoot Them.

- Report feral hog sightings and damage to 573-522-4115, ext. 3296.
- Taking feral hogs is prohibited on conservation areas and other lands owned, leased, or managed by the **M.C.D.** Shooting hogs on other lands is strongly discouraged.

The Conservation Department and the U.S. Department of Agriculture Animal and Plant Health Inspection Service, along with other partners and hundreds of private landowners, are working to eradicate feral hogs in Missouri. Hogs are social animals that travel in groups called sounders. Shooting one or two hogs scatters the sounder and makes trapping efforts aimed at catching the entire group at once more difficult. With their high reproductive rate, removing only one or two hogs does not help to reduce populations. Anyone who observes a feral hog or damage caused by feral hogs should report it to the **M.C.D.** rather than shooting the animal.

GENERAL INFORMATION

Article from an M.D.C publication

VITAL TARGET AREAS

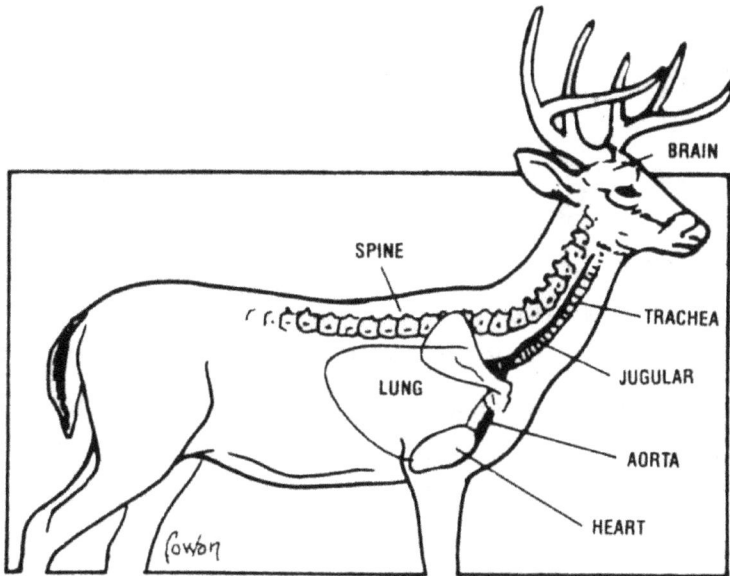

Always be sure that you have a clear shot at a vital area. Shooting a deer any other way could result in a wasteful, inhumane, slow and painful death. A deer's brain, heart, spine, and lung are the primary target areas for a quick, clean kill. Of the four, the brain is the least desirable, for several reasons. The target is small, and if the shot is a little off its mark, the result could be a broken jaw, resulting in a slow agonizing death from starvation or infection. Also, there's the rack to consider. A badly placed head shot could do considerable damage to it. A deer's heart is very low in the chest. If your shot goes low, a clean miss or a broken leg may result. Hitting a deer in the spine is an instant knock down, and if close to the head, death is instantaneous. However, this requires a very accurate shot. The lung is a good target. It's the largest area, and allows for several inches of variance in any direction. A lung shot is a sure kill, but don't be surprised if a deer shot in the heart or lung runs a hundred or more yards before falling. Wait a while before going after it. If a shot misses the heart or lung but damages a main artery, the deer will bleed out, but will probably also run a short distance before it goes down. If you find your deer down, but another shot is necessary, the *coup de grace* should be a spine shot, very close to the head.

Since a deer shot with an arrow will die from hemorrhaging, the heart or lungs are the best targets when bow hunting.

TRAILING A WOUNDED DEER

If a well-hit deer does not go down immediately or gets up and runs after falling, don't hesitate to shoot again if you have a clear shot. Wait a while before looking for your deer. If wounded, a deer probably won't go farther than the nearest cover; but if pursued immediately, it will try to keep moving. A wounded deer is an easy target for other hunters. You'll have a much better chance of finding your deer untagged by someone else if you give it time to run undisturbed.

Occasionally even a mortally wounded deer won't leave a blood trail—it may be bleeding internally. That's why it's important not to give up on finding your deer too soon. Deer have been known to hide under leaves, in brush or in a ditch, if they're being pursued and cannot go on. This little trick has caused hunters to accuse them of vanishing into thin air.

If you find a blood trail, you can tell a lot from the color and condition of the blood. Blood from the lungs will be foamy or frothy, and have a pinkish color. A gut shot deer may have stomach or bowel contents mixed with its blood. Bright red blood indicates arterial bleeding. Blood from a vein is dark, and blood from the heart can look both bright and dark. A deer's four-chambered heart contains both dark and bright red blood at the same time. Blood returning to the heart is depleted of oxygen, making it dark. It is then pumped from the heart to the lungs to be re-oxygenated, and returns to the heart bright red. The heart contains bright red blood in two of its chambers, and dark red in the other two at the same time, which can make it hard to determine exactly where the deer was hit.

ARCHERY

Hunting deer with a bow and arrow is very popular in Missouri for several reasons. For one, the season is longer, giving you more hunting time. Currently, archery season in Missouri runs from September 15th through January 15th, with a brief interruption during the regular firearms season. Another reason is that it's a little less expensive than hunting with a firearm. Current regulations (as of 2017) allow you to take two deer and two turkeys with one tag. Bow hunting is probably safer than hunting during the firearms season. It's a little more challenging, but aside from all that, most of us just enjoy it.

Archery became regulated by the MDC in 1946. That year, seventy-three archers participated in a three day bucks-only hunt in Crawford County. It was four hunting seasons later before the first buck was reportedly killed. Since then, interest in the sport has increased steadily, along with the deer population. As a result of the thousands of dollars that archers and other sports people have provided for the welfare and propagation of wildlife in Missouri, as well as the work done by the MDC and other conservation-minded groups, the whitetail deer herd in Missouri is in good condition, increasing each year for the enjoyment and benefit of hunters and non-hunters alike.

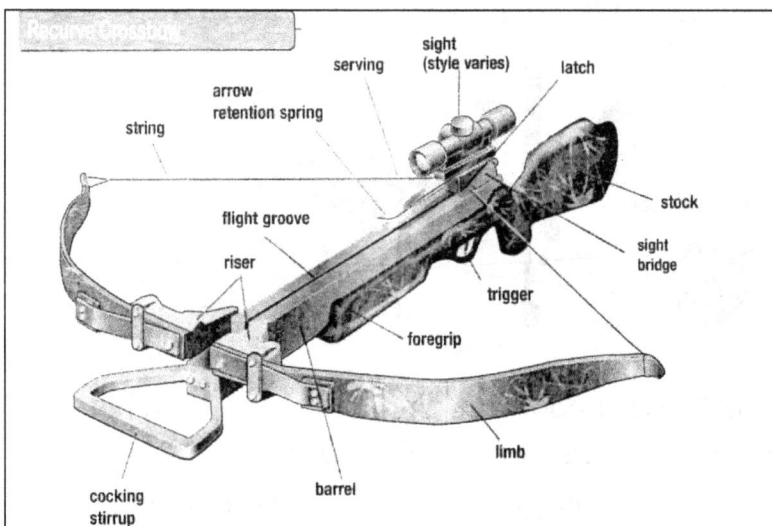

Crossbow

A crossbow is a bow with a rifle-like stock that shoots shorter arrows (sometimes referred to by the medieval term "bolts" or "quarrels").

The four basic bow types are compound, recurve, straight limb and crossbow. Most hunters prefer the compound bow. It's easier to draw and hold, and the arrow travels faster and hits harder than the recurve or straight limb. However, many hunters still prefer to use the recurve bow. The straight-limb bow (long bow) is very seldom used anymore.

Until recently, the crossbow wasn't legal during archery season without a special permit, but that law changed in 2016. Now a crossbow can be used in the archery season with an archery permit, or as a firearm with a firearm permit.

Longbow

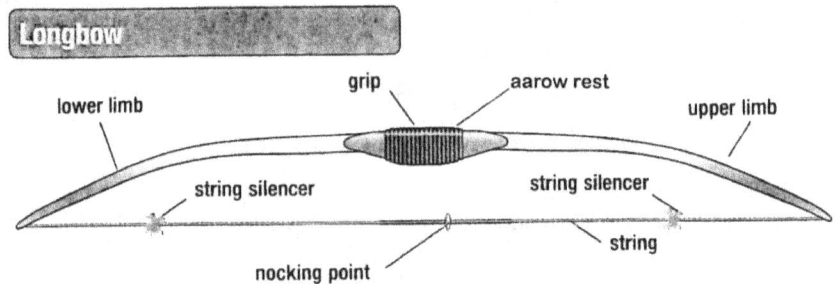

Recurve Bow

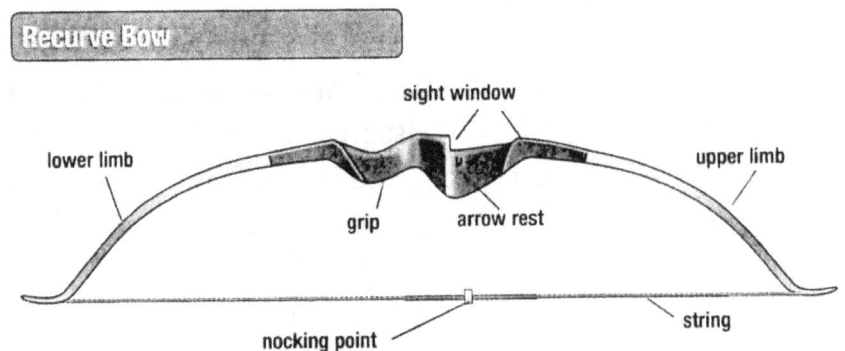

Compound bow

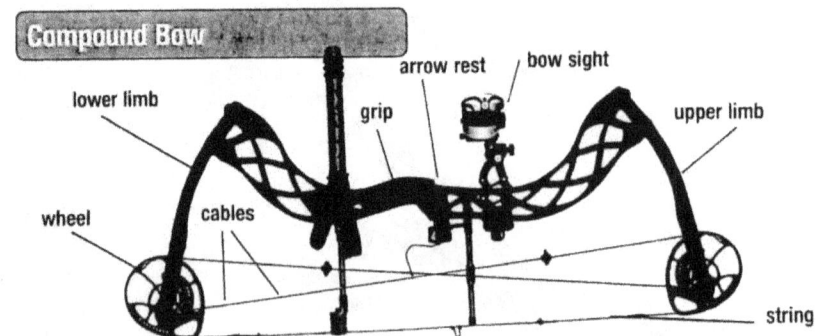

When purchasing archery equipment, it's important that the bow matches the shooter, the arrows match the bow, and you're comfortable with the accessories. Beginners should get help from an expert, or at least a knowledgeable person, to get started, and then practice, practice, practice. Many stores carry inexpensive ready-made targets. Targets can also be made from bales of straw or hay, or a thick sheet of Styrofoam. Brightly-colored fletching on your target arrows can make stray shots easier to find. If you're having trouble getting a consistent pattern when practicing, check the stiffness of the arrows you're using. When an arrow is released from the bow, it flexes before straightening out in flight. If the arrow doesn't have the right stiffness for that particular bow, it cannot produce an accurate shot pattern.

Of the various materials arrows are made of, aluminum was the favorite for many years. Now carbon has taken its place as a more durable choice. Broadheads come in many designs and weights. As with firearms, where you hit the deer is more important than what broadhead you use. Make sure the point you practice with and the broadhead you hunt with are the same weight.

There are many accessories that may be helpful: Sights, wrist guards, shooting gloves, finger tabs, string silencers, stabilizers, arrow releasers, bow holders, brush guards, camouflage bow covers, etc.. A wrist guard not only protects the shooter's arm, it helps keep loose sleeves and other clothing away from the string when it is released. If you plan to carry an extra bowstring, it should be put on the bow and pulled a few times to get it stretched and ready to be used. Have the knock point and other accessories already on the string.

There is currently no regulation for the pull weight of a bow in Missouri. You should be able to pull and hold your bow at full draw for at least five seconds. This may require some exercise. Shooting a bow requires the use of shoulder and back muscles that may seldom be used otherwise, and may need some strengthening. When shooting, find an anchor point that you're comfortable with, such as your chin, cheek, or the corner of your mouth.

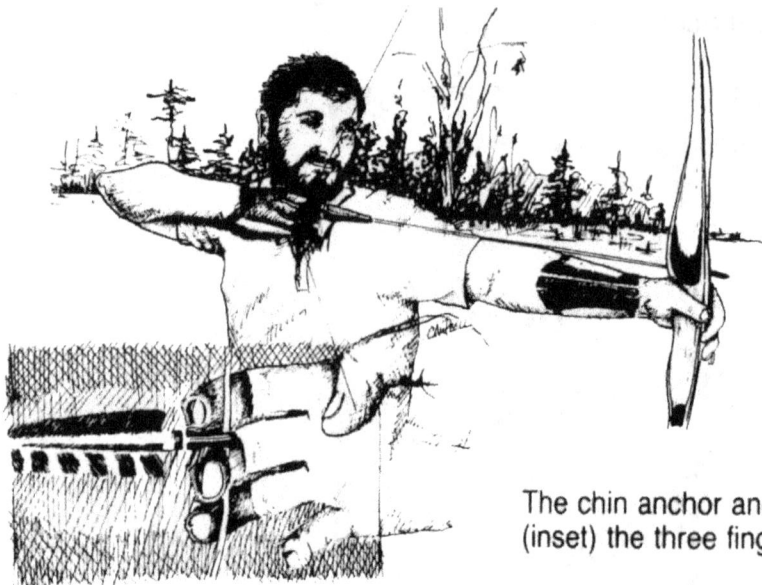

Thumb under chin.

The chin anchor and
(inset) the three finger hold

Regulations are subject to change. Check current "Deer Hunting Information" pamphlet.

The corner of mouth anchor

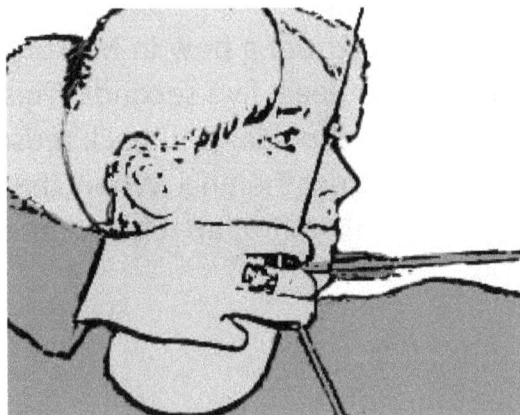

Cheekbone anchor

anchorthatpoint.com

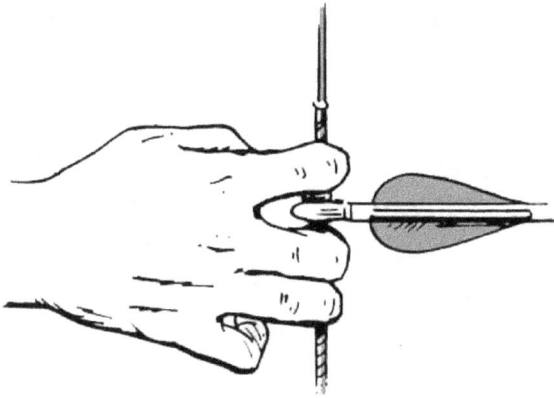

The Correct
Three Finger Pull is
using tips of fingers only.

Never release a fully drawn bow without an arrow in place. This can damage the bow. Let the string go back slowly, with a little tension on it. Bring the bow to full draw each time you shoot. Follow-through is important. Try to hold "on target" for a second or two after releasing your shot, whether shooting a bow or a gun. That will keep you from pulling your sights off-target a split second too soon. Sometimes we are impatient and pull away to see the result of the shot too quickly.

There are several organizations that can help if you have questions—Missouri Bow Hunters, the National Archery Association, and the Fred Bear Sports Club, to name just a few. You can also find help at most sporting goods stores.

When bow hunting, camouflage is the name of the game if you hope to get within shooting range. Even the arrows that you hunt with should be painted camouflage. Wearing faded camouflage clothing is not good. As a rule, the more contrast in your camo, the better. As mentioned in the "Tree Stands" section, hunting from an elevated stand is especially effective when bow hunting.

When shooting a bow, a little twist in your string as you pull tends to hold an arrow in place, but too much twist can affect the flight of your arrow. A peep sight in the string might help prevent this. Check with an archery dealer to get one installed correctly. You can buy a bow holder that hangs from the hunter's waist or attaches to a tree stand, or you can sew a "V" shaped pocket to the bottom of your pant leg, where you can rest the tip of your bow while standing for a long period of time. A piece of string tied to the end of your bow or onto a tree limb can serve as a wind indicator.

When field dressing a deer during archery season, or in any mild weather when insects are active, wiping the cavity with leaves or paper towels will leave a layer of dried blood that can help protect the meat from dirt and insects.

Manufacturers of archery equipment recommend the following care for a bow:

<u>HOYTE EASTON</u>: Do not store a bow where it is subjected to excessive heat. When storing a compound bow for a long period of time (between seasons), release the tension on the limbs by alternately turning the adjustment screws. Keep an exact count

and record the number of turns. Never overdraw or dry fire a bow. Apply a light coating of bowstring wax to the string about once a month, and wax the entire bow every two or three months. Check cables frequently, and replace them if any wear is found.

BEAR ARCHERY: Replace the bowstring yearly, or after 10,000 shots, whichever comes first. Lubricate eccentric wheels and pulleys at the axle; light machine oil is sufficient. Do not oil the cable grooves. Don't grip the bow too tightly when shooing. Bear Archery also recommends not shooting a bow with your hand completely open, or completely closed, unless using a bow holder.

Wrong   Right

THE BLACK WIDOW BOW CO of Highlandville, Missouri, makes excellent recurve bows. According to the company, more recurve bows are damaged while stringing or unstringing than by anything else. A recurve bow can be damaged if not strung properly. Limbs faced and backed with fiberglass can withstand tremendous stress when used properly, but using

Left illustration shows a popular method of stringing a recurved bow. However this method is not recommended by some bow manufacturers.

The use of a bow stringer is easy and a safer way to string a recurved bow.

the "push pull" or "step through" method (as shown) of stringing your bow can cause delamination. They do not recommend unstringing a recurve bow if you're shooting it occasionally. To store a strung bow, hang it horizontally by the string on two pegs. Fiberglass is very durable; however it is sensitive to abrasions and high temperatures. A bow should never be left in a hot vehicle or stored (strung or unstrung) where it will be exposed to extreme heat. Heat softens the resin in fiberglass, and can cause permanent distortion. Never store a bow for a long period of time on one of its limbs. Storing the bow

In a case is best. A coating of bees wax will help protect the bow and bowstring from weather and abrasion. Examine the string periodically for any signs of wear, and replace it if any is found.

FIELD DRESSING YOUR DEER

Never assume a deer is dead just because it's down and not moving. The feet and head of a panicky deer can be dangerous if it suddenly tries to get up. Approach it from behind, and touch the eyeball with a stick or gun barrel. If there's any life in the deer, the eye will blink. If the eyes are closed, be especially careful. . .the deer is probably not dead. If another shot is necessary, place it in the spine close to the head. When you're sure the deer is dead, tag it and start field dressing it to get the body heat out, so the very important cooling process can begin.

To field dress your deer, you will need a sharp knife that is strong enough to cut through the pelvic bone. You'll also need a plastic bag if you want to keep the heart and liver, and paper towels for wiping the cavity (leaves will also work for this). Wiping excess blood & moisture from the cavity will leave a film of dried blood that can protect the meat from dirt and moisture. Some like to wear rubber gloves when field dressing a deer.

See next page for field dressing instructions and illustrations:

Dress deer immediately to insure rapid loss of body heat. Hang animal head up or lay it on a slope with rump lower than shoulders.

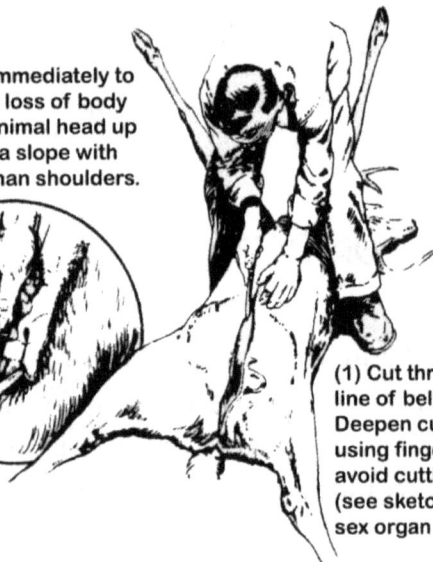

(1) Cut through hide along center line of belly from brisket to vent. Deepen cut through belly muscle using fingers to guide knife and avoid cutting intestines or paunch. (see sketch in circle) Cut around sex organ of buck and remove.

(2) Cut deeply around anus. Remove it with intestines. Separate hind quarters by splitting pelvic bone with sharp, heavy knife or handaxe.

(3) Open chest cavity by splitting the cartilage that joins the ribs to the breast bone. Split muscle (diaphragm) separating chest from stomach cavity

(4) Sever gullet and windpipe as far forward as possible. Pull heart, liver, lungs, paunch and intestines out on the ground. place heart and liver in plastic bag.

(5) Prop body cavity oen with sticks and cool quickly by hanging head up in a shady, airy place. Let it hang this way for about an hour before moving it to camp or car.

Courtesy Missouri Department of Conservation

If you remove the tarsal glands, it should be done after you finish field dressing the deer, to prevent transferring any of the strong-smelling musk from the knife to the meat (some hunters like to place these glands near their stands, if they have more tags to fill). Keep the carcass dry (dampness promotes bacteria), and keep it out of direct sunlight, even in cool weather. Except for being field-dressed, a deer must remain intact until it's checked in.

To determine a deer's live weight using the chart below, measure it around the chest where the heart is (or was), just behind the front legs. Compare that number to the chart. For example, if the measurement is 35 inches, the estimated field-dressed weight is 102 pounds, and the live weight would have been 134 pounds.

Heart girth	Hog-dressed weight		Total body weight	
	Fawns	Adults	Fawns	Adults
in. (cm)	lb. (kg)	lb. (kg)	lb. (kg)	lb. (kg)
20(50.8)	23(10.4)		32(14.5)	
21(53.3)	27(12.2)		37(16.8)	
22(55.9)	31.(14.1)		42(19.1)	
23(58.4)	35(15.9)		48(21.8)	
24(61.0)	39(17.7)	40(18.1)	53(24.1)	62(28.1)
25(63.5)	43(19.5)	46(20.9)	58(26.3)	69(31.3)
26(66.0)	47(21.3)	52(23.6)	64(29.1)	75(34.1)
27(68.6)	51(23.2)	57(25.9)	69(31.3)	82(37.2)
28(71.1)	55(25.0)	63(28.6)	74(33.6)	88(40.0)
29(73.7)	59(26.8)	68(30.9)	80(36.3)	95(43.1)
30(76.2)	63(28.6)	74(33.6)	85(38.6)	102(46.3)
31(78.7)	67(30.4)	80(36.3)	90(40.9)	108(49.0)
32(81.3)	71(32.2)	85(38.6)	95(43.1)	115(52.2)
33(83.8)		91(41.3)		121(54.9)
34(86.4)		96(43.6)		127(57.7)
35(88.9)		102(46.3)		134(60.8)
36(91.4)		108 49.0)		141(64.0)
37(94.0)		113(51.3)		147(66.7)
38(96.5)		119(54.0)		154(69.9)
39(99.1)		124(56.3)		161(73.1)
40(101.6)		130(59.0)		167(75.8)
41(104.1)		136(61.7)		174(79.0)
42(106.7)		141(64.0)		180(81.7)
43(109.2)		147(66.7)		187(84.9)
44(111.8)		152(69.0)		193(87.6)
45(114.3)		158(71.7)		200(90.8)
46(116.8)		164(74.5)		206(93.5)
47(119.4)		169(76.7)		213(96.7)
48(121.9)		175(79.5)		219(99.4)
49(124.5)		180(81.7)		226(102.6)
50(127.0)		186(84.4)		233(105.8)
51(129.5)		192(87.2)		239(108.5)
52(132.1)		197(89.4)		246(111.7)

RELATIONSHIP BETWEEN BODY WEIGHT AND HEART GIRTH IN WHITE-TAILED DEER

In the present report rather few deer of body weight greater that 70 kg were examined In regions where white-tailed deer frequently exceed 70 kg body weight additional observations may be necessary to verify the value of the present regression equations in predicting body weight of large deer.

Courtesy
VIRGINIA POLYTECHNIC INSTITUTE AND STATE UNIVERSITY
Blacksburg, Virginia 24061
COLLEGE O FAGRICULTURE AND LIFE SCIENCES

OUT OF THE WOODS

Man stops when he sees fellow hunters pulling the deer out of the woods incorrectly. He says "You guys are ruining a lot of good meat by dragging him by the back legs. Why don't you pull him by the antlers?"

One replied, "We tried that but we kept getting farther away from our truck."

DUH!

A buck's antlers make good handles for pulling. Drag a doe by her front legs, or tie a rope around her neck and a strong stick to the other end of the rope. If your rifle is not equipped with a sling, a temporary one can be made with rope to free up both your hands. A head lamp is very helpful when dragging a deer after dark. Never carry a deer over your shoulder. That's a good way to get shot at.

If you need to leave a field-dressed deer in the woods temporarily, and you think you may have trouble finding it when you come back, tie a handkerchief or something on a limb where it can be spotted with a flashlight.

Don't get in a hurry when dragging your deer. Some of us are over forty, overweight, and over-dressed. If we're not careful, we might be over with.

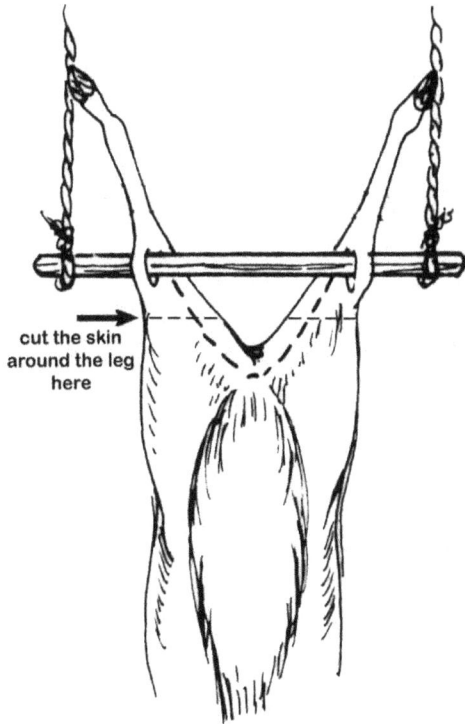

Skinning a Deer

cut the skin around the leg here →

The sooner the hide is removed, the easier it will come off. However, to protect the meat from dirt and insects, the hide should be left on until being processed. To remove the hide, hang the field-dressed deer by its back legs (some prefer to hang them by the head).

If the cape is to be saved for mounting, it should be removed before skinning (for instructions, see the section on mounting). Start skinning from the back legs by cutting around them just below the gambrels. Cut along the dotted lines as shown in the illustration, severing the tail by cutting through the bone where it connects to the body. Pull the hide down, tail included. A few additional cuts may be necessary to free the hide as you pull. Use a spray bottle to spray water on the hair occasionally, to keep it from sticking to the meat during the skinning process.

If you plan to save the hide for tanning, get it to a cool place as quickly as possible. If tanning will be delayed, contact the taxidermist for instructions. You may need to roll up the hide and freeze it

Mounting

Taxidermists are like any other craftsperson. Some do better work than others. If possible, have someone recommend a good one. Two things that are essential to a good head and shoulder mount are getting enough material to work with when you remove the cape, and getting it to the taxidermist in good condition as soon as possible. The processor might remove the cape for you while you wait, since the deer has to be skinned before hanging in the processor's cooler anyway.

Make sure the cut is made behind the front legs. If you remove the cape yourself, start the cut where the neck joins the head, between and just behind the ears (see illustration). Cut along the spine to a few inches behind the shoulders. Cut down both sides just behind the front legs and across the stomach. Make necessary cuts around both legs below the shoulders. Do not make any cuts in the throat area. The cut should be along the top of the neck. Pull the hide down and over the deer's head. The cape should be inside out and lying loosely over the deer's head. Remove the head where it joins the neck. Do not remove the hide from the deer's head. Roll the head and hide together, wrap them in a damp towel, and get them on ice or in a cool place.

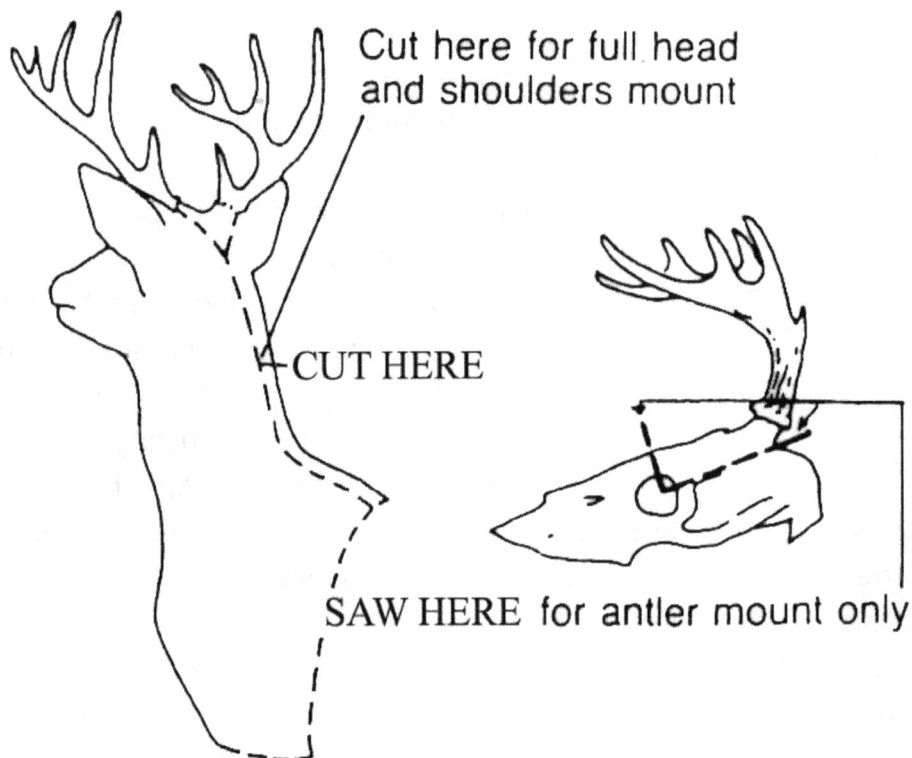

Cut here for full head
and shoulders mount

CUT HERE

SAW HERE for antler mount only

PROCESSING

Even before the hunt begins, it's good to know where you plan to have your deer processed, if you don't intend to do it yourself. Some hunters like to find a processing plant close to their hunting area. They take the deer there directly after the hunt, and later return to pick up the frozen meat.

Let your processor know if you want to save the back straps and tenderloins; otherwise they'll be part of the steaks. You should also have an idea about how much of the deer you want ground into burger, and whether you want pork or beef fat added. Let him know what size you'd like the roasts to be, and how much summer sausage you'd like, if any. Make sure your processor knows if you want to save the cape to be mounted later.

Deer carcasses have been butchered in many ways. The basic two are:
#1   The beef method - bone in
#2   Boning method - de-boned

Using the Beef Method

Split the hanging carcass with a meat saw after removing backstrap and tenderloin. Lay one of the sides on the work table. Start at the front and remove the shoulder by cutting between the fifth and sixth ribs.

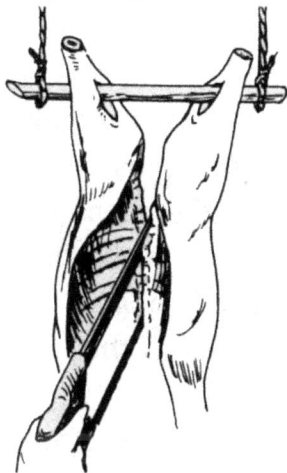

The neck and foreshank should be removed, boned and used for grinding.

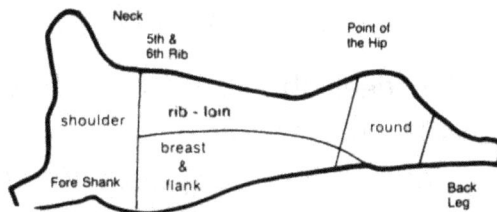

The shoulders make good roast either grilled or roasted. (especially grilled)

Make the next cut at the point of the hip to separate the rib-loin portion from the leg and round. The breast and flank should be removed and used for grinding. The loin-rib section may be cut and the bones sawed to make chops and steaks. If a power saw is not available, **a regular wood saw can be used.** you may want to de-bone it and just slice the meat.

To process the round, remove the pelvic and leg bones and make boneless roasts, steaks or leave it whole to slice when ready to fry. Meat from the back leg can be ground. Some meat can be left on the ribs and back bones for grilling and baking or the bones can be trimmed closely and scrap meat used for grinding.

HOME BUTCHERING

To get the estimated live weight & edible meat, weigh the field dressing carcass and compare to this chart

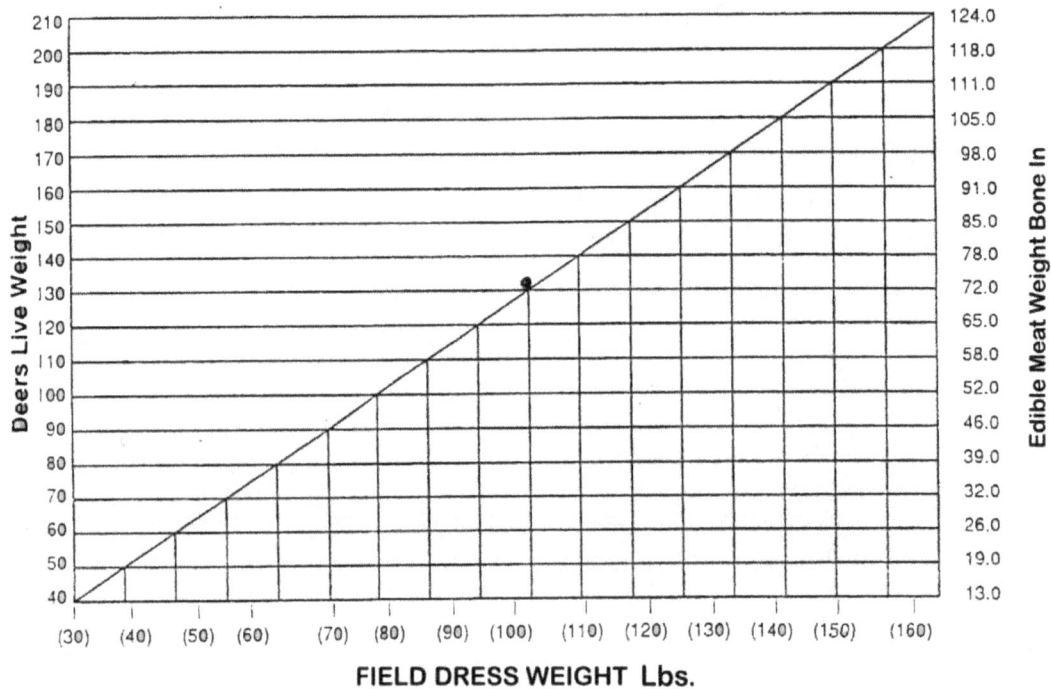

FIELD DRESS WEIGHT Lbs.

A freshly killed deer should be field-dressed, then left undisturbed for about an hour. This allows the meat to firm up before the deer is moved. Unfortunately, this is not often done, and not absolutely necessary for top quality meat. It's just a plus in the all-important early stages of handling a freshly-killed deer. After the meat has set, it should be chilled as quickly as possible. How the carcass is cared for in the first day or two is very important; unfortunately, this is usually when venison gets its worst treatment. Most freshly killed deer are dragged out of the woods when they should be left undisturbed for the meat to set.

During this time they should be cooling, but often they're hung from a tree limb in temperatures that are too warm, and often in direct sunlight. But if you take a reasonable amount of care, a deer will provide good, nutritious, low-calorie and low-fat meat. The chart shows the amount of edible meat that can be obtained from a whitetail deer. For example, a deer with an estimated live weight of 130 pounds (see the chart) weighs approximately 100 pounds after field-dressing, and can produce roughly 72 pounds of edible meat, a little less if it's been de-boned.

There are two basic methods of butchering a deer. The "beef method," also called the "wholesale cuts" method, is the way a butcher or processing plant would do it to make roasts and steaks. The "deboning method," is simpler—you just cut the meat from the bones, making pieces to roast, fry, grill or whatever.

You'll need a large cutting board, sharp knives, a marker for labeling, wrapping paper and tape. Plastic freezer bags also work well. If using the "beef method," you'll need a meat saw (a clean wood saw will work). If you want to save the tenderloins and backstraps, make sure they are removed before sawing through the backbone.

Hang the carcass as shown. After the deer has been skinned, remove the tenderloins and backstraps. The tenderloins are found on each side of the backbone, on the inside of the cavity. The backstraps are larger, attached to the backbone, one on each side, on the outside of the cavity just under the hide. After these delicacies are removed, it helps to split and quarter the deer to make it easier to work with. Remove the shoulders, which make good roasts, either baked or grilled. Meat on the fore-shanks can be removed for grinding. Remove the ribs, which can be grilled, or the meat cut away for grinding. The neck makes a good roast. It should be cut lengthwise, and cleaned out. Cut the remaining meat according to its intended use. The heart, cut open and cleaned out, can be sliced and fried, or baked whole. Deer's liver can be prepared as you would beef liver and onions.

THE DRUGSTORE FOLD is a good method to seal moisture in and air out.

Roll folded edge down, turn package over

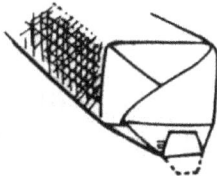

Fold tip of point over

Fold up and tape

The simplest way to freeze your venison is in plastic bags. The more traditional method is to wrap the meat in moisture-proof paper. Place the meat in the center of the paper, then tightly fold the sides and secure with freezer tape. Date and identify each package. When freezing several pieces of meat together, placing a sheet of waxed paper between each piece makes them easier to separate when thawing.

To speed up freezing, separate packages of meat when placing them in the freezer, so cold air can reach all sides. Frozen cuts of venison begin to lose flavor after six to eight months, ground meat a little sooner. Quick-freezing preserves flavor, but unfortunately cannot be done in most home freezers.

HOME TANNING

In the past, the best advice for anyone wanting to try home tanning was "don't do it." Previous methods were complicated, tedious, and quite often unsuccessful. Then the MDC provided a method that was simple and fairly easy, which worked so well that some professional tanners use it. Many products have become available that make home tanning nearly foolproof. For those who are interested in trying it out, the MDC's steps are shown below. If you follow these directions, you should be well-pleased with your finished product.

Step 1: It is very important to remove all flesh and fat from the hide. Scrape the hide with a knife while the skin is still fresh. If you can't work on the hide while it's fresh, freeze it until you're ready, then allow it to thaw. Remove as much flesh and fat as you can, then rub non-iodized salt onto the skin. Roll the hide up, salt–side in, and allow it to set for two or three days. When you unroll the hide, you will find that the salt has loosened any flesh and fat that held fast the first time you scraped the skin.

Step 2: When you have the hide free of all flesh and fat, it's time to de-grease it. Use naphtha thinner, and rub it well into the hair and onto the skin. *Naphtha is highly flammable, so use it outdoors and away from open flame.* After you have worked the naphtha well into the skin, rub sawdust into the hair and onto the skin to absorb the naphtha and dissolved grease. Repeat this three or four times, shaking off the sawdust each time. Rinse the hide very thoroughly to remove any remaining salt, naphtha, or sawdust.

At this point, the hair may be removed from the hide if you desire (if you want to preserve the hide with the hair in place, proceed to Step 3). Hair can be removed by soaking the hide in a solution of hydrated lime, wood ashes, and water (¼ pound hydrated lime, ½ cup wood ashes, and 1 gallon of water). After several days, the hair can be rubbed off or scraped off with a knife. Deer taken in the fall or winter have fully-developed coats, and the hair is usually easier to remove because of its uniform length. Removing the hair from deer hides taken at other times of the year tends to be more difficult, because many small, undeveloped hairs stay in the skin after the longer hairs are scraped off.

After the hair has been removed, rinse the hide in warm water, and place it overnight in a solution of boric acid and water (one ounce boric acid crystals to one gallon water). This neutralizes any hydrated lime left in the skin. After removing the hide from the boric acid solution, rinse it well, and proceed to Step 3.

Step 3: The hide is now ready to go into the tanning solution, where it will stay for seven days. To make the tanning solution, dissolve ½ pound salt and ¼ pound alum per gallon of water, making enough to completely cover the hide. Stir the solution daily. After a week, remove the hide from the solution, rinse it in clear water and allow it to drain, but do not let it dry out. Rub warm neatsfoot oil onto the skin side of the hide, and, while keeping it out of direct sunlight, let the hide start drying out. As it dries, pull and stretch the hide in all directions. A board clamped into a vise provides edges over which you can work the hide back and forth to help with the softening process.

Continue doing this at periodic intervals until the hide is completely dry. If the hide dries too quickly, or you need to leave it for several days during this step and the hide gets stiff, dampen it with a wet sponge until it becomes limp again, and resume manipulation of the hide. When finished, the skin should be white and the hide soft, supple, and ready to use. To remove any remaining tissue or unevenness on the skin side of a finished hide, sand it with a piece of coarse sandpaper (#60 or #80 grit). This will create a suede look to the hide.

When working with the leather, you'll find that skin from a deer's neck is thicker than skin from the back, the skin from the back is thicker than skin from the sides, and belly skin is the thinnest of all. If you desire a uniform thickness, use coarse sandpaper to rub the skin down. A belt sander can also be used to thin a deer hide, but it can take off a lot of material quickly, so be careful.

Plastic buckets are recommended for holding the solutions, and you may want to wear rubber gloves. Chemicals may be purchased locally, and they are available online. When using these chemicals, read and follow all the directions.

CAMPING

For some, camping is a big part of deer hunting, whether for the entire hunt, or just a day or two. Take pictures and make a few notes for the folks back home to laugh at—I mean, look at.

"Be prepared" is a good rule for camping. Be ready for changes in the weather and for increased appetites. Bring more water than you think you'll need. . .you probably *will* need it. If you make ice in gallon milk jugs, you'll have extra water as the ice melts. Know the laws about gathering firewood and burning on government or conservation land. If open fires are allowed, bring a leaf rake to use as a fire-fighting tool in case your campfire gets out of hand.

Don't forget insect repellent, wasp and hornet spray, and a fly swatter, especially if the weather is mild, or if your tent or camper gets warm and some of these critters wake up. You might even bring a mouse trap. If space is limited, dehydrated and powdered food items such as milk, potatoes, and eggs take up less room and don't need to be refrigerated. Take along a carton of wet towels (baby wipes), and a first aid kit. In addition to the usual stuff in the kit, you might want to include a magnifying glass, tweezers, fingernail clippers, and eye drops. Don't forget prescription drugs, allergy medicine, or any other special medication you might need.

Snake bite is always a possibility in mild weather, especially during early archery season. Missouri has five poisonous snakes—the copperhead, cottonmouth, timber rattlesnake, pygmy rattlesnake, and massasauga rattlesnake. If a snake bite occurs, call 911. Keep the victim calm. If the bite is on or near the hand, remove rings and other jewelry before swelling sets in. Keep the injured area below the level of the heart. Do not attempt to catch the snake for identification—you might get bitten again. Some people recommend not washing the wound because any venom left on the skin may help identify the snake, but cleaning the wound is probably a good idea. Applying a tourniquet is not recommended. Do not make any cuts to the wound or apply suction, particularly from your mouth. Do not apply ice to the wound. There are snake bite kits available, but the recommended first aid is to keep the victim calm and get medical help as quickly as possible.

Plants like poison ivy, poison oak and certain sumacs do not need to be leafed out to cause an allergic reaction. People often make contact with these plants while gathering firewood. If you burn wood with poison ivy on it, you can even get an itchy rash from the smoke.

If you're camping out in the open, stay away from trees with dead or broken limbs, which may come down in a strong wind. Also, choose a spot with good drainage in case of heavy rain.

If the weather is warm, you might want to consider putting down a large tarp or sheet of plastic to set the tent table and chairs on. That will help discourage bugs and insects from crawling around.

Things can easily be stolen from an unattended campsite. Anything that cannot be locked up should be put out of sight, or at least covered up when the camp is unoccupied.

CAMPFIRES

Be careful with fire. You may be held liable if a fire gets out of control and causes property damage. Know the regulations about burning in your area. When gathering firewood, try to select wood (such as oak and ash) that makes good coals, and does not shower sparks. Hickory and Osage orange (hedge apple) make a hot fire, but both throw a lot of sparks. These sparks can be a fire hazard. When gathering firewood in National Forests, State Parks, or on land owned or managed by the MDC, only take wood that is already down. Tree cutting is not allowed in these areas without a special permit.

Here are some of the more popular types of camp fires. If you plan to cook over one, it helps to let the flames go down to hot coals. It's easier to control the heat that way.

Kettle Fire

Keyhole Fire

Hunter Fire

WIND

Logs

Hunter Fire

WIND

Rocks

Kettle Fire – for hovering over fire.
Keyhole fire – for cooking on coals.
Hunter fire – both ends open to wind
Star fire – for burning long logs

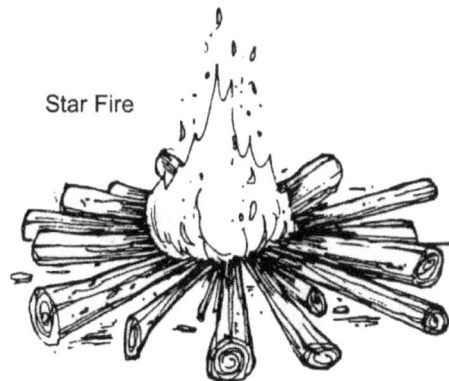

Star Fire

UNFAMILIAR TERRITORY

When entering unfamiliar territory, observe landmarks such as hilltops, towers, power lines, unusual trees or rock formations, and distant buildings or roads. As you walk through the woods, turn around occasionally to see what to look for on the way back. If you become lost, the standard distress signal is three gunshots fired into the air, a few seconds apart. Another is a column of white smoke. To make a smoke column, build a hot fire and lay an armful of weeds, limbs, or leaves (the greener the better) on the flames. That will temporarily smother the fire and produce a column of smoke which can clearly be seen for a long distance.

When you begin to get that "lost" feeling, it helps to just sit down. Sitting has a calming effect. Even if you're over-dressed, too warm or tired, do not discard anything. You'll probably need it later. Listen for sounds such as barking dogs or distant traffic. Make a plan for your comfort and safety in case you have to spend the night in the woods. Gather firewood, clear a space, build the fire and stay by it. If possible, make a lean-to with brush and limbs. Before going into the woods, pack a few things just in case you get lost, such as extra water and shells, matches, snacks (jerky, raisins, chocolate, nuts), a headlamp, compass, whistle, and a large trash bag to sit or lay on. Along with the knife and rope you already have, these will give you a pretty good survival kit. I hate to say it, but a cell phone (turned off while you hunt) can be very useful. If your keys have a button that will flash the lights or honk the horn of your vehicle, that can be helpful as well.

Hunter 1: "I think we're lost."

Hunter 2: "Don't worry, All we have to do is make three shots into the air and we'll be found soon." He shot three times into the air, and no one showed up. Later he shot off three more, and no one came.

Hunter 2: "We're in trouble now. That was my last arrow."

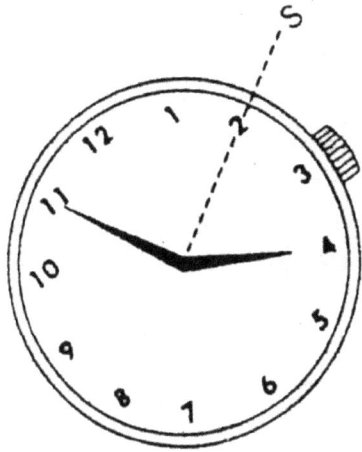

If you want to find directions and the sun is up, you can use your watch as a compass. Hold the watch flat. Point the hour hand at the sun. *South* will be half way between the hour hand and the twelve, going forward or backwards, whichever is the shortest way.

SAFETY

Records show that a large percent of firearm accidents happen in or around the home. Wherever they occur, they usually involve family and friends. Treat all firearms as if they were loaded, until you look and see for yourself. Don't take anyone's word for it—check it yourself. Never point a firearm, loaded or not, at anyone. Never pull a firearm directly toward yourself by the barrel, especially if it's lying flat, like on the seat of a vehicle or the bed of a truck, where the trigger could catch on something. If someone hands you a gun, be sure the barrel is up or down—never right at you or someone else.

Firearms have been known to go off when they slide and hit the ground or floor, so be careful not to lean your gun against a slick surface such as a wall, a bumper, or a vehicle without some side support. When crossing a fence, it might be easier to hold your gun in one hand while you climb, but it's much safer to lay down the gun or let someone hold it while you cross. When pulling your firearm into your tree stand, pull it so that the barrel isn't pointing directly at you. Be aware of what's beyond your target, especially when shooting at a running deer.

VENISON

Game meat: How does it stack up against beef and pork?

Meat (3 ounces lean)	Calories	Fat (grams or g)	Saturated fat	Cholesterol (milligrams or mg)
Deer	128	2 g	1 g	67 mg
Elk	134	2 g	1 g	62 mg
Moose	114	1 g	1 g	66 mg
Beef tenderloin	185	9 g	4 g	71 mg
Pork tenderloin	159	5 g	2 g	80 mg

Source: U.S. Department of Agriculture Nutrient Data Laboratory, 2004

CONTENT PROVIDED BY
MayoClinic.com

Excerpts taken from a study done on feeding habits of the Missouri Whitetail deer.

Four hundred and forty deer stomach contents were collected over a five year period. Samples were taken from all areas of the state from deer killed during the hunting season, and from highway, illegal and other kills during that period of time.

While more samples were available during the fall and early winter hunting season, stomach contents representing each month of the year were examined.

Two hundred twenty two food items were identified in this study. Principal year round foods for the 5 year period by major groups were:

Acorns and Oak leaves	42.5%	Antennaria (Ladies tobacco)	3.1%
Corn	14.3%	Unclassified weeds	2.8%
Coralberry	8.7%	Winter wheat	2.2%
Sumacs	8.4%	Red Cedar	1.4%
Korean Lespedeza	4.3%	Honey Locust	0.8%
Grass and Sedge leaves	3.5%	Miscellaneous	8.0%

(Many food items such as persimmons and other wild fruit, mushrooms, etc. that deer are very fond of are not listed here because they are not considered a principal food)

* In the absence of acorns deer turned to the agricultural crops of corn, lespedeza, wheat, alfalfa, and to the fruits of sumacs, coralberry (the red berries of buckbrush) as their primary source of food.

Venison from a healthy deer is capable of producing low-calorie, low-fat, high protein meat. The poor texture and flavor often associated with it is not always the fault of the venison, but the result of improper handling of the carcass before (and sometimes during) processing. Granted, rutting activity (especially of older bucks) may affect the quality of the meat. Other than that, it would be hard to distinguish between a buck and a doe of similar age, taken from the same area and properly processed. Both will produce high quality meat.

Venison purchased from places licensed to sell it commercially is usually quite a bit more expensive than beef or pork. However, if you choose not to keep the meat from your hunt, you can donate it to the "Share the Harvest" program here in Missouri. They will make very good use of it.

For more information on Share the Harvest

Share the Harvest
Missouri Department of Conservation
P.O. Box 180
Jefferson City, MO 65102-0180
(573) 751-4115
www.missouriconservation.org

Conservation Federation of Missouri
728 West Main
Jefferson City, MO 65101
(573) 634-2322
www.confedmo.com

Share the Harvest sponsors

All frozen meat should be defrosted in a refrigerator. Defrosting at room temperature can promote bacterial growth on the surface before the center is completely thawed. Tough pieces of venison can be tenderized by marinating it for twelve to twenty-four hours in Italian salad dressing, any citrus juice with a little added vinegar, buttermilk, or plain old meat tenderizer. Worcestershire sauce and other steak sauces can be used to tenderize the meat and to improve flavor. Because venison has no marbling (strips of fat within the meat), cooking it with bacon can add both moisture and taste.

In addition to salt and pepper, lemon, garlic, M.S.G. (Accent) and butter are some of the things that enhance the unique flavor of venison. Sweet salads, applesauce and other fruit dishes go very well with venison. Use a good meat thermometer to be sure that your meat is cooked, without it getting over-done and dried out. Look for an internal temperature of 120 to 140 degrees for rare, 140 to 160 degrees for medium, above 160 degrees for well done. Venison is very lean and should not be overcooked. It's usually best just barely well done, and served hot.

Q. What is HONEYMOON *salad?*
A. Lettuce Alone!

RECIPES

VENISON ROAST

2 tablespoons oil
2 pounds venison roast, all fat removed
2-3 strips bacon
1 10.5 ounce can mushroom soup, mixed with one can milk
1 10.5 ounce can beef or chicken broth, or beef bouillon in 1½ cups water
2-3 minced garlic cloves
½ package dry onion soup
3 stalks celery, cut up
3 potatoes, cut up
1 large onion, cut up
4 carrots, cut up
1 cup chopped mushrooms
Salt and pepper to taste\
Accent (MSG—optional)

Oil a 5-quart slow cooker. Place the roast in the cooker, lay the bacon strips on top. Mix the mushroom soup and milk with the broth (or bouillon), the garlic, and the onion soup mix and pour it over the roast. Add the remaining ingredients to the slow cooker. Cover and cook on high for 5-6 hours. You can also place the ingredients in a roasting pan, and cook it in a 300 degree oven for three hours.

VENISON STEW

2-3 pounds of venison, cut into bite-size pieces, all fat removed

6 beef bouillon cubes

4 cups water (more if needed)

4 cups milk

1 medium onion, chopped

3 carrots, cut up

3 stalks celery, cut up

3 medium potatoes, cut up

1 level teaspoon garlic powder

¼ teaspoon nutmeg

Salt & pepper to taste

Approximately 2 tablespoons flour, slightly more if you want a thicker stew

Brown the venison. Combine the remaining ingredients, except for the flour, and add them to the pan. Simmer approximately 1½ hours (adding water as necessary). Remove one cup of liquid and let it cool slightly. Stir in the flour until dissolved, and return the liquid to the pan. Cook and stir until the stew is slightly thickened. This dish can be served over rice or noodles.

VENISON STEAK

Prepare the way you'd prepare a beef steak. Be careful not to overcook the venison; use a meat thermometer to determine doneness.

CHILI ROYALE

2 pounds ground venison

½ pound ground pork sausage (if no pork was added to the venison when it was processed)

2 tablespoons oil

2 15 ounce cans crushed tomatoes, undrained

2 15 ounce cans chili beans, undrained

1 cup chopped green pepper

1 cup chopped onion

4 cups tomato juice

4 tablespoons chili powder

1 bay leaf

3 cups water

2 teaspoons vinegar

1 teaspoon thyme

2 cloves minced garlic or 1 teaspoon garlic powder

½ teaspoon black pepper

Dash cayenne pepper or hot sauce (optional)

Salt, to taste

In a skillet, brown the venison and pork in the oil, breaking into crumbles. Add to a pan with the rest of the ingredients. Simmer, stirring frequently, for half an hour. Remove bay leaf.

BAKED SHOULDER ROAST

1 venison shoulder
Salt, pepper, and garlic powder
2-3 strips bacon
1 package of dry onion soup mix
2 cups water
Flour
1 cup beef broth

Score the top of the roast. Rub in salt, pepper, and garlic powder. Place meat in an oiled roasting pan. Lay the bacon strips across the top. Mix the dry onion soup mix with the water, and add it to the pan. Cover the roast with foil and bake for two hours at 300 degrees, basting occasionally. Add additional water if necessary. Remove the roast from the pan and let it rest for ten minutes before slicing. Add the flour and 1 cup of warm broth to the pan juices to make gravy. Dissolve the flour completely, then bring the mixture to a boil, stirring constantly, until it thickens.

GRILLED SHOULDER ROAST

1 venison shoulder
Salt, pepper, and garlic powder
Barbeque sauce

Prepare coals, or set your gas grill to high heat. Score both sides of the roast. Rub the roast with salt, pepper and garlic powder. Place on the grill, and bake, turning occasionally. Reduce temperature to medium, and grill until a meat thermometer reads 120 to 140 degrees for rare, 140 to 160 degrees for medium, 160 degrees or above for well-done. Cover both sides of the roast with barbeque sauce. Let the meat cook for about one minute longer, being careful not to let the sauce burn. Turn the roast over and cook for another minute. Serve hot, with additional sauce.

VENISON STROGANOFF

3 tablespoons oil
2 pounds venison, sliced thin
½ cup onions, cut in small pieces
1 cup mushrooms, cut up
4 cups water
4 beef bouillon cubes
1 package dry onion soup mix
1 package stroganoff seasoning
2 tablespoons (¼ stick) butter
2 minced garlic cloves, or ½ teaspoon garlic powder
½ teaspoon oregano
2 tablespoons flour, for thickening
2 cups sour cream
½ cup shredded cheese
Salt, pepper and Accent (MSG—optional)
Cooked rice or noodles
Parsley, finely chopped broccoli florets, or chopped green onions, for garnish

Heat oil in a skillet, and brown the venison with the onions and mushrooms. Remove from heat. Bring water to a boil in a medium-sized pan, add bouillon, and stir to dissolve. Add the onion soup mix, stroganoff seasoning, butter, garlic and oregano, stir well. Add the meat mixture. Reduce heat, simmer for about one hour. Remove a cup of the liquid, stir in the flour and return it to the pan. Increase the heat, stirring until the mixture is slightly thickened. Remove from heat. Stir in sour cream and cheese, add salt and pepper to taste. Sprinkle with Accent, if using. Serve over rice or noodles, and garnish with the parsley, broccoli or green onions. Hot bread and sweet salad go very well with this dish.

FRIED HEART

Cut the heart in half. Rinse and remove everything that is not solid meat. Slice the heart into ¼ inch pieces. Dip the pieces into milk or buttermilk. Coat with flour and fry in oil. Season with salt, pepper, and garlic powder to taste.

FRIED LIVER

Deer liver
Lemon juice
2 onions
2 tablespoons butter
½ cup milk
½ cup flour
Butter or oil, for frying
FOR THE GRAVY:
2 tablespoons flour
1 cup milk
1½ beef broth
Salt, pepper, garlic powder and Accent (MSG—optional)

Rinse the liver and cut away any gristle. Slice the liver into ¼ inch-thick pieces. Dampen the pieces with lemon juice and let them set for a few minutes. Slice the onions and sauté them in butter. Set aside. Dip the liver pieces in milk, coat with flour, and fry them over medium heat in butter or oil in a covered skillet. Turn the meat occasionally. Cut into a piece to check for doneness. Do not overcook. Remove the liver from the pan and keep it warm.

To make the gravy, dissolve the flour in the milk, and add it to the pan along with the beef broth. Simmer and stir, scraping up the cooked bits from the bottom of the pan, until gravy is slightly thickened. Add salt, pepper, garlic powder, and Accent (if using). Place the liver slices on a warmed platter, cover with the onions and gravy. Serve hot.

MY FAVORITE

Cut pieces of venison approximately 2x4" and ¼ inch thick
Put them through a tenderizer
Dip in your favorite batter
Fry in hot oil
Salt, pepper, garlic powder and Accent (MSG) *optional

You can make venison jerky by using a dry rub or a marinade. Cut the venison into 1/8 to ¼ inch thick slices. For the dry rub, mix approximately 2 parts salt, 2 parts black pepper, 1 part brown sugar, ¼ part garlic powder and ¼ part MSG (Accent—optional). Sprinkle liberally onto both sides of the meat. Refrigerate for twenty-four hours. If you prefer a marinade, mix 1 cup orange juice or unsweetened grapefruit juice, ¼ cup soy sauce, 4 tablespoons oyster sauce, and 1 teaspoon brown sugar. Place the meat and marinade in a freezer bag or non-metallic dish, and refrigerate for twenty four hours. Drain the marinade, then salt and pepper the slices.

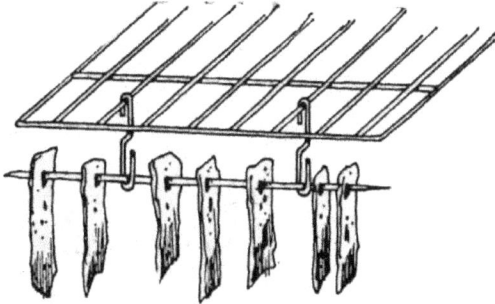

Whether using a dry rub or a marinade, the simplest way to make jerky is to use a dehydrator. If you don't have one, place the meat strips in a 150 degree oven. Lay the slices on the oven racks, hang them with paper clips as shown, or lay them on a cookie sheet. If using a cookie sheet, the slices will need to be turned often.

The time required will vary, but the jerky is done when it is completely dry, while retaining some flexibility.

Do you know why Cannibals won't eat clowns?

They taste funny

CAMPFIRE VENISON ON A STICK

Soak wooden skewers in water (or use metal skewers). Thread bite-size pieces of venison, mushrooms, broccoli, onion, 1-inch pieces of bacon, and green pepper onto a skewer and hold it over the fire until meat is done. Baste with Italian dressing or barbeque sauce occasionally.

SCRAP PILE

Making Scrap Pile is a good way to use up leftovers. The dish will be different every time you make it, and the ingredients will depend on what you have on hand. The amounts and items on the ingredient list can vary, and the dish will still be filling and tasty.

2 tablespoons oil
3 cups chopped vegetables. These can be a combination of chopped onions, mushrooms, broccoli, carrots, or whatever you have.
2 tablespoons butter
2 tablespoons Worcestershire sauce
1 pound venison, cut into bite-sized pieces
Salt and pepper to taste
3 cups cooked rice
¾ cup cheddar cheese

Stir fry the vegetables in the oil until they are tender. Remove from the skillet and keep them warm.

Add the butter and Worcestershire sauce to the skillet. Season the meat with salt and pepper, then cook until it is no longer pink. Return the vegetables to the pan. Add the cooked rice and stir to combine. Sprinkle with cheese, place the lid on the skillet and turn off the heat. Wait a minute for the cheese to melt. This dish is good with soy sauce, hot sauce or additional Worcestershire sauce.

Information in this book was taken (with permission) from the Missouri Department of Conservation, knowledgeable people and personal experiences. I hope you enjoy it. Special thanks to my daughter Kathy, for many hours` helping me with this handbook. To Sharon Kizziah-Holmes of Paperback Press, thank you for being the publishing coordinator on this project. It's been a long time coming, but we made it happen.

Remember that those involved in hunting accidents are very often friends or members of the family, so "think safety", and good hunting.

Ron Goodman

Miscellaneous

Information Available

Even with 95% of the land in the state privately owned, there is still a lot of land available to the public for hunting. The U.S. Forest Service owns approximately 3 million acres, including the one and a half million acres that comprise the Mark Twain National Forest, located in the central and southern part of the state. Most of this land is open for hunting. For information regarding the Mark Twain National Forest, contact the U.S. Department of Agriculture, at www.fs.usda.gov/mtnf.

The Missouri Department of Conservation also has thousands of acres that are available for public hunting. Additional information regarding this public land is available by contacting the MDC, at https://huntfish.mdc.mo.gov.

In addition, there are many publications available to hunters through the MDC, including the monthly magazine, *Missouri Conservationist.* This magazine is available free to adult residents, and features many informative seasonal articles.

For topographical maps of Missouri, contact the Missouri Geological Survey in Rolla, MO, or visit https://dnr.mo.gov/geology.

For information regarding the Hunter Safety Program, and other programs offered by the MDC, visit https://mdc.mo.gov, or stop by a local office.

Conservation Dept. Offices

Central Region
3500 East Gans Road
Columbia, MO 65201
573-815-7900

Kansas City Region
12405 SE Ranson Road
Lee's Summit, MO 64082
816-622-0900

Northeast Region
3500 S. Baltimore
Kirksville, MO 63501
660-785-2420

Northwest Region
701 James McCarthy Drive
St. Joseph, MO 64507
816-271-3100

Ozark Region
551 Joe Jones Blvd.
West Plains, MO 65775
417-256-7161

Southeast Region
2302 County Park Drive
Cape Girardeau, MO 63701
573-290-5730

Southwest Region
2630 N. Mayfair
Springfield, MO 65803
417-895-6880

St. Louis Region
2360 Highway D
St. Charles, MO 63304
636-441-4554

How to Measure a Rack

WHITETAIL and COUES DEER

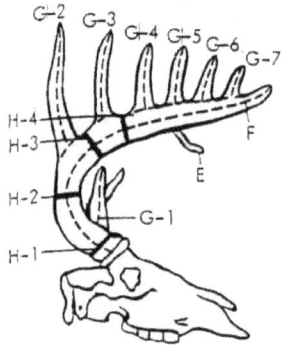

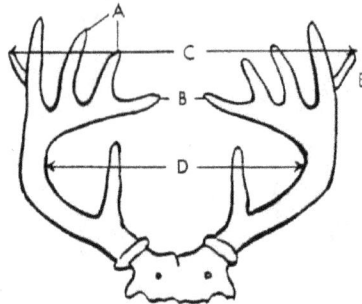

KIND of DEER _____

Detail of Point Measurement

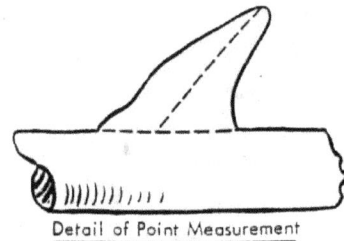

See Other Side for Instructions	Supplementary Data		Column 1	Column 2	Column 3	Column 4
	R.	L.	Spread Credit	Right Antler	Left Antler	Difference
A. Number of Points on Each Antler						
B. Tip to Tip Spread						
C. Greatest Spread						
D. Inside Spread of Main Beams		Spread credit may equal but not exceed length of longer antler				
If Inside Spread of Main Beams exceeds longer antler length, enter difference						
E. Total of Lengths of all Abnormal Points						
F. Length of Main Beam						
G-1 Length of First Point, if present						
G-2 Length of Second Point						
G-3 Length of Third Point						
G-4 Length of Fourth Point, if present						
G-5 Length of Fifth Point, if present						
G-6 Length of Sixth Point, if present						
G-7 Length of Seventh Point, if present						
H-1 Circumference at Smallest Place Between Burr and First Point						
H-2 Circumference at Smallest Place Between First and Second Points						
H-3 Circumference at Smallest Place Between Second and Third Points						
H-4 Circumference at Smallest Place between Third and Fourth Points or halfway between Third Point and Beam Tip if Fourth Point is missing						
Totals						

Add	Column 1		Exact Locality where killed
	Column 2		Date Killed By whom killed
	Column 3		Present owner
Total			Address
Subtract Column 4			Guide's Name and Address
Final Score			Remarks: (Mention any abnormalities)

Courtesy Boone and Crockett Club.

Official scoring system for North American big-game trophies—whitetail and coues deer.

TRUE OR FALSE

1. It is legal to use a crossbow during archery season.

2. Camouflage-patterned hunter orange garments (hat and coat or vest) meet the clothing requirements during firearms season.

3. When counting antler points, both sides of a whitetail's rack are counted, but only one side of a mule deer's rack is counted.

4. Normally, whitetail bucks shed their antlers and grow new ones every year.

5. For deer hunting in Missouri, muzzle loading (alternate method) rifles must be .40 caliber or larger.

6. Shed antlers are often consumed by squirrels, mice, and other rodents.

7. Whitetail does that are pregnant for the first time normally have one fawn. Twins are common after that.

8. According to the Department of Conservation, Missouri's deer herd is currently over a million animals.

9. It is legal to cool a freshly-field dressed deer in any body of water.

10. Whitetail fawns are never capable of participating in the rut in their first year.

11. Whitetails north of the Missouri River are usually larger than deer south of the river.

12. Deer killed in Missouri must be checked in the same day.

13. Whitetail bucks often collect a harem of does during the rut.

14. Unless hit in the spine, a mortally wounded deer may run a hundred yards or more before falling.

15. Currently, Missouri claims the #1 non-typical whitetail rack and the #3 typical whitetail rack in North America.

16. Landowners using their Special Hunting permits do not need to tag and check in their kills.

17. A dog may be used to find a downed deer, but special rules apply.

18. Current first aid for snake bite is keep the victim calm, do not make cuts on the bite, do not apply a tourniquet, and get the person professional medical help as quickly as possible.

19. Most firearm accidents involve friends or members of the family.

20. When on a deer stand, try to keep the wind and the sun hitting your back

ANSWERS
1. True
2. False
3. True
4. True
5. True
6. True
7. True
8. True
9. False
10. False
11. True
12. True
13. False
14. True
15. True
16. False
17. True
18. True
19. True
20. False

The following excerpt was taken from an article written by a self-proclaimed "dyed in the wool" animal lover. It's important to note that there's a big difference between a non-hunter and someone who's anti-hunting, and I think the non-hunter who penned this article did a good job of describing the difference between the two.

A NON-HUNTER LOOKS AT HUNTING

Author Unknown

Hunting is an emotionally-charged issue, and everyone seems to have strong opinions about it. People know exactly where they stand on the subject, but seldom can they tell you exactly how they came to their conclusions. Hunting is such an emotional issue that people think of it in very black and white terms. They love animals, so they hate hunting. Or they love the outdoors, so they love hunting. The truth is that there are many different types of hunting, and many different reasons to do it. Some of the motivations are inexcusable, others are necessary. I don't hunt, but I have to accept the fact that some of the reasons to hunt are honorable, and in the long run, in the best interest of the species involved. I understand all the arguments that animal lovers have against hunting and I respect their opinions, but I cannot be categorically opposed to hunting. Common sense won't stand for it.

What I hope to do here is to explain why I, a dyed-in-the-wool animal lover, cannot be anti-hunting. It's not because I think my opinions are so valuable, but hopefully to give other non-hunters a little comfort with the knowledge that at least some forms of hunting are actually beneficial for animals; and whatever their individual motivations, hunters, as a group, do more good than bad for wildlife.

I'm going to focus on animals that are commonly hunted in Missouri, particularly deer. Anyone who's ever watched Bambi search for his mother after she bravely draws the fire of the deer hunters gets a twinge of sadness every autumn when thousands of these hunters enter the woods in search of the gentle, helpless creatures that live there. Some people get more than a little twinge of sorrow, they get absolutely incensed. If they knew the truth, they would understand that, like it or not, deer hunting is one of the most beneficial forms of hunting practiced today. Anyone who enjoys occasionally spotting a deer should thank a hunter. The whitetail deer population has greatly increased over the past hundred years, mainly due to the efforts of the Missouri Department of Conservation, funded in part by hunting license fees. Deer management has resulted in a healthier herd. Hunting may decrease the number of deer in an area, but the deer that are left benefit greatly. For instance, there have been studies indicating that more deer have twins in areas that permit hunting than in areas that do not.

Hunters don't necessarily hunt to benefit the deer; that's just the icing on the cake. People may hunt to get meat, but frankly that's a lot cheaper and easier to obtain from a grocery store. People choose to hunt because it's *fun.* That really bothers anti-hunters...how can anyone enjoy killing an animal? But for most hunters, the killing isn't what they enjoy. It's the hunt itself, the entire hunting experience, the forest, the campfire, the cold wet autumn air, and the lasting friendships formed around a kerosene lantern. It's not entirely important whether or not their hunt is successful, most hunters just enjoy the time spent in the woods. As long as people who choose to hunt do so in a humane fashion, following the laws and regulations established by the Missouri Department of Conservation, I have no problem with this form of escape.

Although anti-hunters know why they dislike the activity, they may not have thought their arguments though. Some of the more common complaints are listed below. Just a few facts might be enough to turn an angry anti-hunter into simply a non-hunter.

Hunting in Unnecessary

In the past, coyotes, wolves and bears took care of the old, weak, and sick animals in this part of the country. However, in the last few decades, many wild animals have experienced a population explosion, notably whitetail deer. Predation alone could never control a deer herd the size we have in Missouri. If nature lovers want to continue seeing deer in parks, meadows, along roadsides and in camping areas, human management is necessary, and that almost invariably means hunting.

Hunting is Unfair

Until recently, only 10-15% of all hunters were successful during the firearms season. That percentage has risen steadily due to increasing numbers of both deer and hunters in Missouri, but even in an unusually successful year, more than half the hunters who enter the woods come back empty-handed. Things tend to even out in the wilderness: Hunters go in with modern weapons and techniques, and deer use thousands of years of adaptations to evade them.

Animals Killed by Hunters Die Cruelly

Many anti-hunters believe that hunters kill deer cruelly. It's true that it's difficult to gently take a life. But domestic animals are controlled their entire lives by humans, and are killed more cruelly than most hunted animals. If you look at the lives, from birth to death, of both domestic food animals and wild animals, it becomes clear that wild animals lead far more peaceful, natural, and therefore, more satisfying lives than food animals. Deer live in seclusion, going where they please, eating, fighting, mating and raising their own young. The odds are in their favor when hunting season begins, and if a deer is killed, its death is usually less traumatic than that of a domestic animal, if only because it dies fairly abruptly and in familiar surroundings. There are no cramped cages, feedlots, or slaughterhouses, all things that domestic food animals must endure. Anyone who's opposed to hunting out of sympathy for the deer destined for the table, and yet doesn't maintain a strictly vegan lifestyle, clearly has not thought their argument through.

How can a hunter kill an animal as intelligent, beautiful and majestic as a deer?

Many people use this as their main objection to hunting, that they "just couldn't kill an animal with such big soft eyes, or something as cute as a rabbit, or as social as a goose or a duck!" It's probably true that most people would feel squeamish at the thought of killing any animal, which is great. However, aren't we lucky that there are people who are willing to do the dirty work of providing for society? After all, cows have big soft eyes too, and pigs are as smart as dogs. Nothing is more social than a chicken, and all animal babies are cute. The truth is, we don't decide a creature is edible based only on its appearance or lack of intelligence. People who refuse to eat red meat have good intentions where animals are concerned, but it's very nearly impossible to avoid using or consuming *anything* that didn't come from a slaughtered animal. Those cute, smart, friendly domestic animals have endured a great deal at the hands of humans, while deer, and other wild animals, may well die without ever seeing the hunter who shot them, and they die after a life they've lived as they pleased.

Children are taught that hunting is bad at an early age. Everyone knows that Bambi's mother is killed by a hunter, and so are many other animals in the Felix Salten novel. There are adults who say that they became opposed to hunting after watching "Bambi" as a child. Were they equally moved by Pongo and Perdita's anguish at the loss of their puppies in "101 Dalmatians?" Few people vow to keep every puppy their dogs produce, although (if you believe Disney movies), the parent dogs may never recover from their loss. Too many people are just fine with dropping unwanted pets at a shelter, even after seeing the mournful dogs howling the song "Home Sweet Home" at the pound in "Lady and the Tramp." But since most people don't hunt anyway, watching "Bambi" at age five is reason enough to consider all hunting—and hunters—barbaric. Reasonable people simply cannot form strong, lifelong opinions based on the anthropomorphized books or movies they encountered in their youth. As children grow, it's important to give them a realistic and fact-based view of the lives of animals. That should include respect and concern for wildlife, as well as an understanding that hunting is a necessary practice.

To prefer one form of life over another is called "speciesism." All life, no matter what body it's housed in, is a miracle, even in its least impressive form. Everyone kills things, but when it's a pretty or pleasing animal being killed, it's easy for those not doing the actual killing to get indignant about it. Setting a mouse trap is as deadly as setting a wolf trap, and spraying your dog with flea killer can deplete the world of dozens of tiny lives. Hunters aren't the only ones who kill innocent creatures, but they're among the few who replace what they kill, and who regulate themselves so that they kill only at times when the animal population can best withstand it.

No group has done more for wildlife, national forests, and freshwater streams than outdoorsmen. People who don't hunt or fish, and very few of the ones who do, actually, are aware of the positive impact these activities have on conservation. Through licensing fees, special taxes on equipment, and memberships in outdoors organizations, hunters contribute hundreds of millions of dollars each year to conservation. In 1937, The Pittman-Robertson Act (formally known as the Federal Aid in Wildlife Restoration Act of 1937) was signed into law. It created an 11% tax on firearms and ammunition. Originally, the money went to the U.S. Treasury, but after several amendments, Pittman-Robertson funds are now allocated to the Secretary of the Interior.

The money is divided among the states, and how much each one receives is determined by both the size of the state and the number of licensed hunters it contains. The money can only be used by a state's Fish and Game Department, for such projects as land acquisition, habitat improvement, or herd management. Once a project is approved, Pittman-Robinson funds will pay up to 75% of the cost, with the remaining 25% coming from hunting license fees. Any money not spent within two years is turned over to the Migratory Bird Conservation Commission, for the purchase and creation of waterfowl refuges. In the 1970s, the Act was amended to include an 11% tax on archery equipment as well. Since its implementation, the Pittman-Robertson Act has generated over two billion dollars for wildlife.

Of course, hunters don't just buy guns, ammunition and archery equipment. They buy clothes, camping supplies, and lots of food and drinks to bring along. Some buy vehicles, some pay for guides, they buy land to hunt on, and pay for processing, taxidermy, travel, and countless other services and supplies. It's been estimated that when everything hunters purchase is added up, it comes to around ten billion dollars a year. One study found that hunters provide around three and a half million dollars a day to conservation by the purchase of taxable items, and generate up to 324 million dollars a year in Pittman-Robertson funds alone.

Some of the better-known hunter-supported conservation groups include Ducks Unlimited (with 700,000 members; 90 % of those are hunters), the Boone and Crockett Club (a proponent of "Fair Chase," which promotes the ethical, sportsmanlike, and lawful hunting of North American wildlife in a way that does not give the hunter an unfair advantage), The National Wildlife Federation (which was responsible for the passage of the Pittman-Robertson Act), and the Izaak Walton League (which preserves habitat and promotes hunting and fishing as family traditions). There are dozens more organizations, working to increase knowledge, protect wilderness areas, and to preserve this country's hunting heritage. Several species of wildlife were on the verge of extinction, and were brought back from the brink directly through the efforts of these organizations.

Population of Whitetail Deer in MO

Currently there are well over 1,000.000

Anti-hunters often don't see the big picture when it comes to the lives of animals. Some vegetarians don't think twice about buying leather boots for tramping around in the woods, sleeping under down comforters, or giving rawhide chew toys to their dogs. If people who are anti-hunting directed more energy towards demanding better conditions for domestic food animals, they could bring about changes that would improve the lives of millions of animals worldwide, animals whose brief lives are immeasurably worse than those who live as nature intended.

I'm not trying to promote hunting, merely defend it; and to encourage animal lovers, whose hearts are squarely in the right place, to pay closer attention to the animals that truly need their help. They are everywhere, living in factory farms, puppy mills, certain laboratories and on the streets of every city in America. Those are the animals whose lives and deaths should make us angry. Standing up for them is the best way to defend and protect the creatures that we animal lovers care about so much.